Survey of Academic Library Plans for Computer Workstations, Personal Computers, Laptops and Other Computing Devices

ISBN: 978-1-57440-249-0
Library of Congress Control Number: 2013946856

Table of Contents

Survey Participants

Antelope Valley College Library
Arizona State University Libraries
Austin Community College - Library Services
Brooklyn College Library
Buena Vista University
Carl B. Ylvisaker Library
Columbia Basin College
Connors State College
Cuyhoga Community College - East Campus Library
Dar Al-Hekma College Library
Dine College Library
Florida Keys Community College
Frank E Gannett Memorial Library
Grand Rapids Community College
James E. Tobin Library
James W. Miller Learning Resources Center
Knight-Capron Library
Las Positas College
Learning Resource Center - IADT Las Vegas
Loyola Notre Dame Library
McKillop Library
McMillen Library at Indiana Tech
Mount Saint Mary College
Muscatine Community College
Northeast Lakeview Library
Pfeiffer Library
Salisbury University
Shawnee Community College
South Dakota State University Library
Texas A&M University Libraries
University Library
University of Hawaii at Manoa Hamilton Library
University of Wisconsin-River Falls
West Chester University
West Valley College

The Questionnaire

1. How many personal computers does the library deploy in all library locations? Exclude laptops and tablet computers which we ask about separately. Include all computer workstations including those used by library staff.
2. Of the total stock of personal computers deployed by the library, what percentage are for each of the following groups:
   - Primarily for Staff of the Library
   - Primarily for Library Patrons
3. How many personal computers or individual workstations did the library purchase in 2012?
4. How many personal computers or workstations does the library plan to purchase in 2013?
5. Does the library's strategic technology plan call for "turning over' or replacing the library's stock of computers within a certain number of years?
6. If so, how many years is this average "turn over" or replacement cycle for the personal computers used in the library as stipulated in plans and as actually practiced?
   - Planned computer turn over cycle
   - Planned computer turn over cycle
7. What percentage of the computers and workstations that the library plans to purchase in the next two years are:
   - Made by Apple
   - IBM or IBM clones that use Windows/Vista operating system
   - Other
8. Approximately how much did the library spend for personal computers and workstations in the past year, the 2012-13 academic year?
9. How much does the library (or the college in its name) plan to spend on personal computers in the upcoming 2013-14 academic year?
10. What brand of personal computer has the library favored in recent years and why?
11. How many laptop computers did the library purchase in the past year?
12. What is the library's total stock of laptop computers including those for librarians and other personnel as well as for patrons?
13. Of the total number of laptops how many are for library patrons and how many for staff?
14. If you have had losses due to theft of laptops or other mobile computing devices what is the total replacement cost for the items lost? (even if you did not replace them)
15. How much did the library spend in the past year (the 2012-13 academic year) on the following types of technology?
    - Laptops
    - Tablet Computers
    - Netbooks
16. How much will the library spend in the next year, the 2013-14 academic year, on the following types of technology?
    - Laptops

- Tablet Computers
- Netbooks

17. How many computers does the library have that can dual boot Apple and Microsoft operating systems?
18. How many dual-boot computers able to run both Apple and Windows software does it plan to purchase over the next year?
19. Describe your computer tablet purchasing plans. Do you plan to make any such purchases for your library? Which vendors are you considering and why? How do you think it will impact computer use at the library?
20. Describe your laptop purchasing plans. Do you plan to purchase more laptops in the future than you have in the past? Will laptops or tablets start to erode your purchases of fixed workstations?
21. Which brands of laptop has your library preferred in recent years and why?
22. What is the library's total stock of dedicated eBook reading devices (exclude general computer workstations and laptops).
23. How much did (will) the library spend on eBook reading devices in the years specified:
    - 2012-13
    - 2013-14 (anticipated)
24. Does the library current own or lease any of the following
    - Amazon Kindle
    - Sony Reader
    - Barnes & Noble Nook
25. Does the library plan to purchase any of the following over the next two years?
    - Amazon Kindle
    - Sony Reader
    - Barnes & Noble Nook
26. How many of the following does the library (or Information Technology Department if it controls this function) employ on the library technology help desk:
    - Full Time Staffers
    - Part Time Staffers
27. What is total estimated spending for the total annual salaries of full and part time staffers for the library technology help desk?
28. Compare the ease of maintenance of desktop computers with laptop and tablet computers? Which are the most difficult to maintain? Over which do you incur the most maintenance costs in dollars and staff time? Are there hidden costs or savings in deploying one type of computer over another? Or one brand over another? Explain.
29. Rate the following tools for the extent to which they help the library to educate patrons about computer technology in the library.
    - Videos made by the library about library computer technology
    - Videos made by manufacturers about their products
    - Online tutorials made by the library
    - Distribution of training or technology information through social networking sites such as Facebook and Twitter
    - Use of a library technology blog
    - Formal classes for students on library technology

- Print hand-outs describing library technology
- Virtual reference systems or instant messaging

30. If your library outsources any computer or workstation information technology functions, such as maintenance or repairs, describe why you do this and what results that you have achieved. Point out savings in cost or increases in effectiveness. Do you use outside workstation maintenance services?
31. Does your library have one or more computer centers or information technology centers in the library?
32. In your library or library system, how many complexes of computers or workstations would you say might be described as "information commons" or "computer centers" of some kind?
33. Do you think that your library will be increasing or decreasing the number of these centers over the next few years? Increasing their resources or reducing them? What is your philosophy on their development? Will you stand pat? Make major change? How have tablets, netbooks and laptops affected your computer centers?
34. How heavily are your computer centers used? What are the most popular types of hardware and software?
35. Describe how you evaluate the success of a computer center, and how you go about making decisions on new technologies or applications, or entirely new centers.
36. Over the next two or three years does your library plan to replace fixed workstations with laptops or tablet computers? Do you feel the latter are too fragile, prone to theft or unreliable to carry a large part of the end user workstation workload? Does their flexibility offset these often perceived disadvantages? What do you think of the trade offs?
37. Which phrase best describes the library's efforts to make library resources available through tablets, smartphones and other hand held technologies:
    - We have not done much in this area
    - We have not done much but are studying it and plan to do more soon
    - We have already made some provisions for access to some library resources through tablets and smartphones
    - We have numerous applications in place for library resource access through many different types of tablets and smartphones
38. How much has the library spent on smartphone technology in the past two years? How much do you think you will spend cumulatively over the next two years:
    - Past two years
    - Next two years
39. What is your library's peak use period for computer workstations and what do you do during these times, if anything, to serve patrons as best you can?
40. In the following years, approximately what percentage of library patrons predominantly use their own computers while at the library rather than those supplied by the library itself?
    - 2011-12
    - 2012-13
41. For how many mobile devices is the library capable of providing both electricity and internet access?

42. Going forward how do you anticipate that use of patron's own mobile devices in the library will impact your library's computer purchasing plans?

Characteristics of the Sample

Overall sample size: 35

Broken out by level of authority when making decisions about the purchase of new computer technologies:
Recommend only: 13
Need approval: 11
Have authority to buy: 11

Broken out by Carnegie Class
Community College: 14
4-Year College: 6
MA/PHD Granting Institution: 10
Research University: 5

Broken out by Public Versus Private
Public: 24
Private: 11

Broken out by Total Annual Enrollment
2,000 or less: 8
2,000 – 10,000: 16
More than 10,000: 11

Broken out by Total Annual Tuition
Less than $5,000: 13
$5,000 - $20,000: 10
More than $20,000: 12

turn over cycle of 5.4 years. 5.2 years is the average turn over cycle for colleges with 2,000 or less students versus 4.4 years for colleges with 2,000 to 10,000 students.

Plans to Purchase Various Brands of Computers and Workstations

We asked the participants what percentage of the computers and workstations that the library plans to purchase in the next two years are Apple, IBM or IBM clones that use Windows/Vista operating system, and other technology types.

Plans to Purchase Computers and Workstations Made by Apple

Only 3.7% of the computers and workstations that the libraries plan to purchase in the next two years are made by Apple. This includes 5.44% of libraries with a participant who has the authority to buy computers, 7.5% of computers purchased by libraries of research universities, and 4.5% of public college libraries, the highest percentages in their respective categories. The percentage of computers purchased from Apple increased with the enrollment count of each college: colleges with 2,000 or less students plan to purchase 1.33% of their computers from Apple, which increased to 6.67% of computers from colleges with more than 10,000 students enrolled. Economies of scale in purchasing seem to be a significantly factor in purchasing from Apple, whose products generally more more expensive than IBM clones and other personal computer technologies.

Plans to Purchase Computers and Workstations that are IBM or IBM clones that use Windows/Vista operating system

75.38% of the computers and workstations that the libraries plan to purchase over the next two years are IBM or IBM clones that use Windows/Vista operating system. This includes 95.45% of libraries with a participant who has the authority to buy computers, 95.13% of MA/PHD granting institutions, and 75.88% of private schools, the highest percentages in their respective categories. 62.9% of the computers purchased by colleges with a tuition cost of less than $5,000 will be IBM or IBM clones, versus 96% of colleges with a tuition cost of $5,000 to $20,000.

Plans to Purchase Other Computers and Workstations

8.29% of the computers and workstations that the libraries plan to purchase over the next two years are neither IBM clones nor Apple products. This includes 13.57% of the purchases of libraries with a participant who can recommend purchases only, 31.67% of 4-year colleges, and 23.57% of private colleges, the highest percentages in their respective categories. Colleges with a tuition cost of less than $5,000 plan to purchase none of their computers while colleges with a tuition cost of more than $20,000 plan to purchase 23% of computers from other brands. The data shows some marked inconsistencies here and it appears that smaller colleges interviewed did not always understand the questions about operating systems and did not fully appreciate what they were buying. This led to a mistakenly high estimate of the percentage of computers purchased that were neither Apple nor Windows/Vista.

Spending on Personal Computers and Workstations in 2012-13

We asked the participants how much their library spent on personal computers and workstations in the past 2012-13 academic year and the average amount was $17,193.33. Libraries with a participant who could recommend purchases only spent $3,263.64 on personal computers and workstations while libraries with a participant who has the authority to buy computers spent $38,827.27. Research universities spent $79,180 while 4-year colleges spent $3,000. Private colleges spent only $1,987.50 on personal computers and workstations as opposed to public colleges, which spent $22,722.73. Colleges with more than 10,000 students spent $46,590, a significantly larger amount than that of colleges with 10,000 students or less.

Anticipated Spending on Personal Computers and Workstations in 2013-14

The libraries anticipate spending an average of $26,206.32 on personal computers and workstations in the 2013-14 academic year. Libraries with a participant who needs approval before purchasing anticipate spending only $6,434.63 while libraries with a participant who has the authority to buy computers expect to spend $57,033.33. Research universities plan to spend $97,200 while 4-year colleges anticipate their spending to be only $3,694.25. Colleges with 2,000 to 10,000 students anticipate spending $1,888.82 on computers and workstations while colleges with more than 10,000 students expect to spend $68,200.

Preferred Laptop Brands

We asked the participants which laptop brands their library preferred in recent years and why. A majority of the libraries used Dell because this was the only option they had due to a contract they had with their IT department. Dell's were also favored because of their affordability and reliability. Several libraries preferred HP, and a few mentioned Lenovo and Toshiba.

The libraries purchased an average of 5.12 laptop computers in the past year. Libraries with a participant who has the authority to buy computers purchased 11.18 computers, a substantially larger amount than those of the other types in its category. Research universities bought an average of 20.6 computers while 4-year colleges only purchased 1.6. Public colleges purchased 6.29 computers while private colleges bought 2.3. The number of purchased computers increased with the enrollment count of each college: colleges with 2,000 students or less bought only .5 computers, which increased to 12.82 computers for colleges with more than 10,000 students.

The average total stock of laptop computers for the libraries in the sample was 38.21. This includes 71.36 for libraries with a participant who has the authority to buy computers, 93.8 for research universities, and 49.61 for public colleges, the highest numbers in their respective categories. The total stock increased with the enrollment count of the college: colleges with 2,000 students or less had only 3 laptops, which increased to 82.5 laptops for colleges with more than 10,000 students. Colleges with an annual tuition cost of $5,000 to $20,000 had an average stock of 70.5 laptops while colleges with a tuition cost of less than $5,000 had 17.33 laptops.

Number of Computers Reserved for Library Patrons

Of the total number of laptops, the libraries reserve an average of 32.64 (about 75%) for library patrons. Libraries with a participant who needs approval before purchasing reserve only 10.1 laptops for patrons while libraries with a participant who has the authority to buy computers reserve 57.82. 71.2 laptops are available for patrons at research universities while only 11.33 are reserved at 4-year colleges. Public colleges reserve an average of 43.86 laptops while private colleges reserve 10.18. The number of laptops available for library patrons increased with the enrollment count of each college: colleges with 2,000 students or less reserved only 2 laptops for patrons, which increased to 75.44 for colleges with more than 10,000 students.

Number of Laptops Reserved for Library Staff

The average number of laptops available for library staff was 6.76. Libraries with a participant who needs approval before purchasing reserved only 1.5 laptops for staff while libraries with a participant who has the authority to buy computers reserved 13.64. Research university libraries set aside an average of 22.6 laptops for library staff. 8 laptops are available for staff at public colleges versus 4.27 for private colleges. The number of laptops available for library staff increased with the enrollment count of each college: colleges with 2,000 students or less reserved only 1.13 laptops for library staff, and this figure increased to 16.22 for colleges with more than 10,000 students.

Replacement Cost for Lost or Stolen Laptops

We asked the survey participants what the total replacement cost was if they have had losses due to theft of laptops or other mobile computing devices. The average replacement cost was $1,058. The replacement cost for libraries with a participant who needs approval before purchasing was $200 while the replacement cost for libraries with a participant who has the authority to buy computers was $2,580. The average cost for MA/PHD granting institutions was $2,100 while research universities had a replacement cost of only $300. Colleges with a 2,000 to 10,000 students enrolled had a replacement cost of $440 versus $1,757.14 for colleges with more than 10,000 students enrolled.

Spending on Laptops

The libraries sampled spent an average of $4,863.64 on laptops in the 2012-13 academic year. Libraries with a participant who has the authority to buy computers spent $11,118.18 while libraries with a participant who needs approval before purchasing spent only $1,490 on laptops. Research universities spent an average of $20,800 on laptops, a significantly larger amount that those of the other category types. Public colleges spent $6,150 on laptops versus private colleges which only spent $1,433.33. The amount spent on laptops increased with the number of students enrolled at each college: colleges with 2,000 students or less spent $537.50 on laptops, which increased to $13,027.27 for colleges with more than 10,000 students.

Spending on Tablet Computers

The libraries spent an average of $1,039.12 on tablet computers in the 2012-13 academic year. Libraries with a participant who needs approval before purchasing spent only $340 on tablet computers while libraries with a participant who had the authority to buy computers spent $2,236.36. 4-year colleges spent $0 while research universities spent $3,260. Public colleges spent $1,288.75 on laptops versus private colleges, which only spent an average of $440. The amount spent on tablet computers increased with the enrollment count of each college: colleges with 2,000 or fewer students spent only $168.75, which increased to $2,407 for colleges with more than 10,000 students.

Spending on Netbooks

The libraries spent $0 on netbooks in the 2012-13 academic year.

Anticipated Spending on Laptops for 2013-14

The libraries anticipate spending an average of $18,927.23 on laptops for 2013-14., a huge increase over the prior year, nearly a four fold increase. Libraries with a participant who can recommend purchases only expect to spend $27,291 on laptops while libraries with a participant who needs approval for purchasing anticipate their spending to be only $2,679.67. Research universities anticipate spending $42,000 on laptops, a significantly larger amount than those of the other category types. Public colleges expect to spend $24,440.91 while private colleges anticipate only $3,764.63 to be spent. Colleges with more than 10,000 students enrolled expect to spend $59,444.44, a substantially higher amount than that of colleges with 10,000 students or less.

Anticipated Spending On Tablet Computers for 2013-14

The libraries anticipate spending an average of $1,552.57 on tablet computers for 2013-14, once again a very large increase, about 50%, over the past year. Libraries with a participant who can recommend purchases only expect to spend only $308.33 while libraries with a participant who has the authority to buy computers anticipate their spending to be $3,144.44. Research universities sampled expect to spend an average of $5,860 on tablet computers, a substantially larger amount than those of the other category types. Anticipated spending of tablet computers increased with the enrollment count of each college: colleges with 2,000 students or less expect to spend only $125, which increased to $3,344.44 for colleges with more than 10,000 students enrolled.

Anticipated Spending on Netbooks for 2013-14

The libraries anticipate spending $0 on netbooks for 2013-14.

Dual-Boot Computers

The libraries sampled have an average of 3.86 computers which can dual-boot Apple and Microsoft operating systems. Libraries with a participant who can recommend purchases only have only .62 dual-boot computers while libraries with a participant who has the authority to buy computers have 9.09 of these computers. Research universities have 7 dual-boot computers versus only 1.14 for community colleges. Public colleges have 4.88 while private colleges have an average of 1.64.

The libraries plan to purchase an average of 0.35 dual-boot computers over the next year. The collective average did nor vary much by type of college or other variable: every library and college type planned to purchase an average of less than 1 dual-boot computers, with the exception of research universities, which expect to purchase 1.25.

Computer Tablet Purchasing Plans

We asked the survey participants to describe their computer tablet purchasing plans, specifically if they plan to make any such purchases for their library and which vendors they are considering and why. We also asked them if they thought it would impact computer use at their library. A majority of the libraries have no plans to purchase any more computer tablets in the upcoming year. On library is purchasing tablets primarily for staff productivity, specifically Apple and Google for their ease of use/updating. The most common choice for a brand was Apple, followed by Kindles. Many of the participants expect that their purchases will have little impact on their library and that a large number of patrons will continue to use their own mobile computing devices rather than one provided by the library.

EBook Reading Devices

We asked the survey participant what their library's total stock of dedicated eBook reading devices was, and the average stock was 3.66. Libraries with a participant who needs approval before purchasing had an average stock of only .73 devices while libraries with a participant who has the authority to buy computers had 7.27. 4-year colleges had 8.5 reading devices, the largest amount in its respective category. Public colleges had 2.75 reading devices while private colleges had 5.64. Colleges with 2,000 to 10,000 students only had .69 reading devices while colleges with 2,000 students or less had 7.

Spending on eBook Reading Devices

The libraries spent an average of $165.79 on eBook reading devices in 2012-13. Libraries with a participant who can recommend purchases only spent $319.31 while libraries with a participant who has the authority buy computers spent only $40. 4-year colleges spent $0 while research universities spent $300. The average spending was $88 for colleges with 2,000 to 10,000 students versus $305.10 for colleges with more than 10,000 students. Colleges with a tuition cost of $5,000 to $20,000 spent $77.78 on eBook reading devices while colleges with a tuition cost of less than $5,000 spent $265.46.

Anticipated Spending on eBook Reading Devices

The libraries anticipate spending an average of $226.47 on eBook reading devices in 2013-14. Libraries with a participant who can recommend purchases only expect to spend only $38.46 on eBook reading devices while libraries with a participant who has the authority to buy computers anticipate their spending to be $540. MA/PHD granting institutions will spend $0 as opposed to 4-year colleges which will spend $833.33. Private colleges anticipate spending $454.55 on reading devices while public colleges expect to spend $117.39. Colleges with 2,000 students or less anticipate their spending to be $812.50 versus $0 for colleges with 2,000 to 10,000 students.

Owning or Leasing an Amazon Kindle

We asked the survey participants if their library currently owned or leased an Amazon Kindle and 31.43% of the libraries do. This includes 38.46% of libraries with a participant who can recommend purchases only, 83.33% of 4-year colleges and 72.73% of private colleges, the highest percentages in their respective categories. 63.64% of colleges with more than 10,000 students enrolled and 33.33% of colleges with a tuition cost of more than $20,000 also own or lease an Amazon Kindle, the highest percentages in their respective categories.

Owning or Leasing a Barnes & Noble Nook

17.14% of the libraries currently own or lease a Barnes & Noble Nook. This includes 23.08% of libraries with a participant who can recommend purchases only, 40% of research universities, and 20.83% of public colleges, the highest percentages in their respective categories. This also includes 36.36% of colleges with more than 10,000 students enrolled, a higher percentage than that of colleges with 10,000 or fewer students.

Plans to Purchase an Amazon Kindle over the Next Two Years

Only 5.71% of the libraries plan to purchase an Amazon Kindle over the next two years. This includes 9.09% of libraries with a participant who needs approval before purchasing, 20% of research universities, and 8.33% of public colleges, the highest percentages in their respective categories. 15.38% of colleges with a tuition cost of less than $5,000 plan to purchase an Amazon Kindle over the next two years versus 0% of colleges with an annual tuition of $5,000 or more.

Plans to Purchase a Sony Reader Over the Next Two Years

Only 2.86% of the libraries plan to purchase a Sony Reader over the next two years. This includes 9.09% of libraries with a participant who needs approval before purchasing, 20% of research universities, and 4.17% of public universities, the highest percentages in their respective categories. 0% of colleges with 10,000 students or less enrolled plan to purchase a Sony Reader over the next two years versus 9.09% of colleges with more than 10,000 students enrolled.

Plans to Purchase a Barnes & Noble Nook

2.86% of the libraries plan to purchase a Barnes & Noble Nook over the next two years. This includes 9.09% of libraries with a participant who needs approval before purchasing, 20% of research universities, 9.09% of colleges with more than 10,000 students, 7.69% of colleges with a tuition cost of less than $5,000 and 4.17% of public colleges, while the rest of the category types were 0%.

Part Time and Full Time Staffers on the Technology Help Desk

We asked the survey participants how many full time staffers their library employed on the library technology help desk. The average number was 2.04. 4-year colleges employed an average of 1 full time staffer while research universities employed 3.4. Public colleges employed 2.4 while private colleges employed 0.83. Colleges with more than 10,000 students employed 4.1 full time staffers.

The libraries sampled employed an average of 6.83 part time staffers on the technology help desk. Libraries with a participant who has the authority to buy computers employed 19.86 and MA/PHD granting institutions employed 23.83 part time staffers, significantly higher amounts than those of the other types in their respective categories. Public colleges employed 9.43 part time staffers while private colleges employed only 1.63. Colleges with 2,000 students or less employed only 0.54 while colleges with more than 10,000 students employed 24.17.

We asked the survey participants what the estimated spending for the total annual salaries of full and part time staffers for the technology help desk was, and the average was $99,352.75. Libraries with a participant who needs approval before purchasing spent $34,011 while libraries with the authority to buy computers spent $186,500. 4-year colleges only spent $28,763.75 while research universities spent $232,500 on full time and part time staffers for the technology help desk. Public colleges spent $133,714.29 versus only $19,175.83 for private colleges. Colleges with 2,000 to 10,000 students spent $14,175.83 on the annual salaries of full and part time staffers while colleges with more than 10,000 students spent $278,333.33.

Maintenance of Laptops Versus Desktops

We asked the survey participants to compare the ease of maintenance of desktop computers with laptop and tablet computers, specifically which are more difficult to maintain and which results in more maintenance costs and staff time. We also asked if there are hidden costs or savings in deploying one type of computer or brand over another. An overwhelming majority of the libraries mentioned that laptops require more maintenance and cost more. The laptops have to be cleaned and inspected, can have faulty wireless connections, and are used more neglectfully by patrons because of their mobility. On the other hand, desktops are easier to upgrade and repair.

Usefulness of Various Tools

We asked the survey participants to rate the following tools for the extent to which they help the library to educate patrons about computer technology in the library: videos made by the library, videos made by the manufacturers about their products, online tutorials, distribution of training or technology information through social networking sites, library technology blogs, formal classes for students on library technology, print handouts, and virtual reference systems or instant messaging.

Usefulness of Videos Made by the Library About Library Computer Technology

28.57% of the libraries found videos made by the library about library computer technology to be very useful. This includes 36.36% of libraries with a participant who needs approval before purchasing, 42.86% of community colleges, 31.25% of colleges with 2,000 to 10,000 students, and 29.17% of public colleges, the highest percentages in their respective categories. Additionally, 37.5% of colleges with 2,000 students or less, 50% of 4-year colleges, and 30.77% of colleges with a tuition of less than $5,000 felt that videos made by the library about library computer technology were useful.

Usefulness of Videos Made by Manufacturers About Their Products

20% of the libraries rated videos made by manufacturers about their products to be very useful. This includes 27.27% of libraries with a participant who has the authority to buy computers, 40% of research universities, 20.83% of public colleges, and 27.27% of colleges with more than 10,000 students enrolled, the highest percentages in their respective categories. Additionally, 50% of colleges with 2,000 students or less, 46.15% of colleges with a tuition of less than $5,000, and 42.86% of community colleges found videos made by manufacturers about their products to be useful.

Usefulness of Online Tutorials Made by the Library

22.86% of the libraries surveyed found online tutorials made by the library to be very useful. This includes 30.77% of libraries with a participant who can recommend purchases only, 40% of research universities, 25% of public colleges, and 30.77% of colleges with a tuition cost of less than $5,000, the highest percentages in their respective categories. Additionally, 25% of colleges with a tuition cost of more than $20,000, 37.5% of colleges with 2,000 students or less, and 50% of 4-year colleges felt that online tutorials made by the library were useful.

Usefulness of Distribution of Training or Technology Information through Social Networking Sites Such As Facebook and Twitter

20% of the libraries agreed that distribution of training or technology information through social networking sites was very useful in educating patrons about library technology. This includes 33.33% of 4-year colleges, 27.27% of private colleges, and 30.77% of colleges with a tuition cost of less than $5,000, the highest percentages in their respective categories. Additionally, 41.67% of colleges with a tuition cost of more than $20,000, 37.5% of colleges with 2,000 students or less, 33.33% of public colleges, and 40% of research universities felt that distribution of training or technology information through social networking sites was useful.

Usefulness of a Library Technology Blog

Library technology blogs were found to be very useful by 14.29% of the libraries surveyed. This includes 18.18% of libraries with a participant who needs approval before purchasing, 28.57% of community colleges, 25% of colleges with 2,000 students or less, and 23.08% of colleges with a tuition cost of less than $5,000, the highest percentages in their respective categories. In addition, 20% of colleges with a tuition cost of $5,000 to $20,000, 20% of MA/PHD granting institutions, and 18.18% of libraries with a participant who has the authority to purchase computers agreed that a library technology blog was useful.

Usefulness of Formal Classes for Students on Library Technology

22.86% of the libraries felt that formal classes for students on library technology were very useful. This includes 27.27% of libraries with a participant who has the authority to buy computers, 40% of research universities, 25% of public colleges and 36.36% of colleges with more than 10,000 students, the highest percentages in their respective categories. Additionally, 25% of colleges with a tuition cost of more than $20,000, 25% of colleges with 2,000 students or less, and 27.27% of private colleges agreed that formal classes for students on library technology were useful.

Usefulness of Print Handouts Describing Library Technology

Print handouts describing library technology were thought to be very useful by 22.86% of the libraries surveyed. This includes 45.45% of libraries with a participant who needs approval before purchasing, 35.71% of community colleges, 25 % of public colleges and 46.15% of colleges with a tuition cost of less than $5,000, the highest percentages in their respective categories. 50% of colleges with a tuition cost of $5,000 to $20,000, 54.55% of colleges with more than 10,000 students and 45.83% of public colleges felt that print handouts describing library technology were useful.

Usefulness of Virtual Reference Systems or Instant Messaging

14.29% of the libraries felt virtual reference systems or instant messaging to be very useful in information literacy and computer instruction tasks. This includes 23.08% of libraries with a participant who can recommend purchases only, 25% of colleges with 2,000 students or less, and 25% of colleges with a tuition cost of more than $20,000, the highest percentages in their respective categories. 30.77% of colleges with a tuition cost of less than $5,000, 27.27% of colleges with more than 10,000 students, 25% of public colleges and 33.33% of 4-year colleges agreed that virtual reference systems or instant messaging were useful.

Outsourcing Maintenance Services

We asked the survey participants if their library outsources any computer or workstation information technology functions and why they do this and what results they have achieved. One library outsources about 95% of their public workstations to a central IT shop on campus which provides a common environment for students across campus with more accessibility to applications and software at a lesser cost.

Information Technology Centers

We asked the participants if their library had one or more computer centers or information technology centers in the library, and 65.71% of the libraries did. This includes 72.73% of libraries with a participant who has the authority to buy computers, 85.71% of community colleges, 79.17% of public colleges, and 84.62% of colleges with a tuition cost of less than $5,000, the highest percentages in their respective categories. On the other hand, 50% of colleges with a tuition cost of more than $20,000 and 54.55% of private colleges do not have one or more computer centers in their libraries.

"Information Commons" or "Computer Center" Complexes

The libraries had an average of 21.93 complexes of computers or workstations that would be described as "information commons" or "computer centers." Libraries with a participant who has the authority to buy computers had 52.4 complexes and MA/PHD granting institutions had 56.78, substantially larger amounts than those of the other types in their respective categories. 4-year colleges had only 4.4 complexes. Public colleges had 29.9 complexes while private colleges had an average of only 3.33. Colleges with 2,000 students or fewer had only 1.71 complexes, which increased drastically to 59 for colleges with more than 10,000 students.

We asked the participants if they thought their library will be increasing or decreasing the number of these centers over the next few years as well as increasing or decreasing their resources for them, and what their philosophy was on their development. We also asked how tablets, netbooks and laptops have affected their computer centers. One library will be creating a research commons that will include a substantial number of computers. Another library will be shifting to the information commons in the next 10 years and away from the computer centers. A few libraries will maintain their current number of computers due to space and budget limitations.

Popular Hardware and Software

We asked the participants how heavily their computer centers were used and what were their most popular types of hardware and software.. Almost all of the libraries' computer centers were used heavily: patrons use the computers every day, and according to one library, particularly in between classes. Popular types of hardware and software included Dell, Apple, Microsoft Office, PowerPoint, Excel, Adobe, Firefox and Safari.

Evaluating the Success of a Computer Center

We asked the participants to describe how they evaluate the success of a computer center and how they go about making decisions on new technologies or applications. Nearly all of the libraries evaluate the success of their computer centers by tracking patron usage. If particular software is heavily used, a library will try to make it available in more locations. The libraries also determine needs of the patrons through surveys. A few of the libraries had little to no control over their purchases because they were determined by their IT department.

Plans to Replace Fixed Workstations with Laptops or Tablets

We asked the participants if their library plans to replace fixed workstations with laptops or tablet computers over the next two or three years, whether they felt laptops were too fragile, prone to theft, or unreliable to carry a large part of the end user workstation workload. A majority of the libraries plan to stay with fixed workstations, stating that all of the mentioned risks of laptops were significant factors in their purchasing decisions. Other libraries mentioned the challenge that laptops pose for students working in groups because of the small screen as well as their inability to run large programs. One library plans to have laptops for librarians and PCs for the rest of the library staff and patrons. Nonetheless, our data shows that – around the margins – laptop use is beginning to impact pc and workstation use in academic libraries, and should emerge as a factor limiting workstation demand, not by displacing workstations, but by absorbing some of the increased computing load and cutting workstation procurement in the future.

Literacy Efforts in Promoting the Availability of Library Content through Hand Held Technology

We asked the survey participants to describe their efforts in making library resources available through tablets, smartphones and other hand held technologies. Response options included that they have not done much in this area, that they have not done much but are studying it and plan to do more soon, that they have already made some provisions for access to some library resources through tablets and smartphones, or that they have numerous applications in place to allow for library resource access through many different types of tablets and smartphones. A plurality of 48.57% of the libraries stated that they have already made some provisions for access to some library resources through tablets and smartphones. This includes 61.54% of libraries with a participant who can recommend purchases only, 60% of research universities and of MA/PHD granting institutions, 56.25% of colleges with 2,000 to 10,000 students and 54.55% of private colleges, the highest percentages in their respective categories. On the other hand, 50% of community colleges, 35.71% of community colleges, and 50% of colleges with 2,000 students or less have not done much in this area.

Spending on Smartphone Technology

We asked the survey participants how much their library has spent on smartphone technology in the past two years and how much they think they will spend cumulatively over the next two years. The average amount spent in the past two years was $578.67. Libraries with a participant who has the authority to buy computers spent $2,215 while libraries with a participant who needs approval before purchasing spent $0. Research universities spent $3,750. Public colleges spent $826.67 while private colleges spent $0. The amount spent on smartphone technology increased with the enrollment count of each college: colleges with 2,000 or less students enrolled spent only $43.75 which increased to $1,667.78 for libraries with more than 10,000 students.

Anticipated Spending on Smartphone Technology

The libraries in the sample anticipate spending an average of $943.08 on smartphone technology over the next two years. Libraries with a participant who has the authority to buy computers expect to spend $3,000, a significantly larger amount than those of the other types in the category. Research universities anticipate their spending to be $5,000 while 4-year colleges expect to spend $0. $1,226 is the average anticipated spending for public colleges versus $0 for private colleges. The anticipated spending of smartphone technology increased with the total enrollment of the college: colleges with 2,000 students or less expect to spend only $62.50, which increased to $2,224.44 for colleges with more than 10,000 students.

Peak Hours for Computers

We asked the survey participants what was their library's peak use period for computer workstations and what they do during these times to serve patrons. The answers varied: responses included both mornings and nights, but a majority of the libraries' computers were used most heavily in the time starting immediately after school until closing, specifically during the weekdays. Finals week is also one of the more crowded times for many of the libraries. The libraries take measurements to assist the patrons, particularly students, by having many printers available, one or several staff members accessible for help, and priority computer usage for students.

Usage of Personal Computers

We asked the participants approximately what percentage of library patrons predominantly use their own computers while at the library rather than those supplied by the library itself in the years 2011 and 2012-13.

Personal Computer Usage in 2011

25.72% of library patrons used their own computers in the library in 2011. This includes 38.13% of patrons from libraries with a participant who needs approval before purchasing, 33.33% of patrons from MA/PHD granting institutions, 36.25% of patrons from private colleges, and 32.78% of patrons from colleges with a tuition cost of more than $20,000, the highest percentages using their own computers in their respective categories.

Personal Computer Usage in 2012-13

34.1% of library patrons used their own computers in the library in 2012-13. This includes 41.67% of patrons from libraries with a participant who needs approval before purchasing, 40.56% of patrons from MA/PHD granting institutions, 42.78% of patrons from private colleges and 39% of patrons from colleges with a tuition cost of more than $20,000, the highest percentages in their respective categories.

Electricity and Internet Access

We asked the participants how many mobile devices their library is capable of providing both electricity and internet access for and the average amount was 2,142.47. This includes 9,757.5 from libraries with a participant who has the authority to buy computers, 6,075 from research universities, 3,117.31 from public colleges, and 5,737.14 from colleges with more than 10,000 students, the highest amounts in their respective categories.

Impact of Personally Owned Mobile Devices on Use of Library Computers

We asked the participants how they anticipated the use of patron's personal mobile devices in the library will impact their library's computer purchasing plans. A majority of the libraries responded that it will lead to a decrease in purchasing computers. One library plans to replace existing workstations but add more seating and electrical service for mobile devices and another library plans to buy large monitors which students can use with their own devices. However, a number of libraries have yet to see a significant impact. Additionally, several libraries serve low income areas; they anticipate that not many of the students will be able to have their own devices.

Chapter 1. Workstations & Personal Computers

Table 1.1 How many personal computers does the library deploy in all library locations? Exclude laptops and tablet computers which we ask about separately. Include all computer workstations including those used by library staff.

	Mean	Median	Minimum	Maximum
Entire sample	183.17	90.00	2.00	1200.00

Table 1.2 How many personal computers does the library deploy in all library locations? Exclude laptops and tablet computers which we ask about separately. Include all computer workstations including those used by library staff. Broken out by Level of authority when making decisions about the purchase of new computer technologies

Level of authority when making decisions about the purchase of new computer technologies	Mean	Median	Minimum	Maximum
Recommend only	88.15	80.00	2.00	310.00
Need approval	72.27	66.00	13.00	149.00
Have authority to buy	406.36	250.00	49.00	1200.00

Table 1.3 How many personal computers does the library deploy in all library locations? Exclude laptops and tablet computers which we ask about separately. Include all computer workstations including those used by library staff. Broken out by Carnegie Class

Carnegie Class	Mean	Median	Minimum	Maximum
Community College	86.64	56.00	13.00	310.00
4-Year College	87.17	85.00	50.00	149.00
MA/PHD Granting Institution	182.20	87.50	2.00	811.00
Research University	570.60	443.00	75.00	1200.00

Table 1.4 How many personal computers does the library deploy in all library locations? Exclude laptops and tablet computers which we ask about separately. Include all computer workstations including those used by library staff. Broken out by Public Versus Private

Public Versus Private	Mean	Median	Minimum	Maximum
Public	235.79	100.00	13.00	1200.00
Private	68.36	66.00	2.00	149.00

Table 1.5 How many personal computers does the library deploy in all library locations? Exclude laptops and tablet computers which we ask about separately. Include all computer workstations including those used by library staff. Broken out by Total Annual Enrollment

Total Annual Enrollment	Mean	Median	Minimum	Maximum
2,000 or less	45.88	41.50	13.00	113.00
2,000 – 10,000	82.00	85.00	2.00	149.00
More than 10,000	430.18	310.00	48.00	1200.00

Table 1.6 How many personal computers does the library deploy in all library locations? Exclude laptops and tablet computers which we ask about separately. Include all computer workstations including those used by library staff. Broken out by Total Annual Tuition

Total Annual Tuition	Mean	Median	Minimum	Maximum
Less than $5,000	89.23	62.00	13.00	310.00
$5,000 - $20,000	364.20	189.50	34.00	1200.00
More than $20,000	134.08	77.50	2.00	811.00

Table 2 OF the total stock of personal computers deployed by the library, what percentage is for each of the following groups: The answers to this question should be a percentage of 100%.

Table 2.1.1 Percentage of personal computers that are Primarily for Staff of the Library

	Mean	Median	Minimum	Maximum
Entire sample	27.57%	25.00%	7.00%	80.00%

Table 2.1.2 Percentage of personal computers that are Primarily for Staff of the Library Broken out by Level of authority when making decisions about the purchase of new computer technologies

Level of authority when making decisions about the purchase of new computer technologies	Mean	Median	Minimum	Maximum
Recommend only	21.15%	16.00%	7.00%	50.00%
Need approval	29.27%	27.00%	7.00%	80.00%
Have authority to buy	33.45%	25.00%	10.00%	68.00%

Table 2.1.3 Percentage of personal computers that are Primarily for Staff of the Library Broken out by Carnegie Class

Carnegie Class	Mean	Median	Minimum	Maximum
Community College	19.36%	18.00%	7.00%	45.00%
4-Year College	32.67%	25.00%	10.00%	80.00%
MA/PHD Granting Institution	25.00%	25.00%	10.00%	50.00%
Research University	49.60%	50.00%	30.00%	68.00%

Table 2.1.4 Percentage of personal computers that are Primarily for Staff of the Library Broken out by Public Versus Private

Public Versus Private	Mean	Median	Minimum	Maximum
Public	26.83%	24.50%	7.00%	68.00%
Private	29.18%	25.00%	10.00%	80.00%

Table 2.1.5 Percentage of personal computers that are Primarily for Staff of the Library Broken out by Total Annual Enrollment

Total Annual Enrollment	Mean	Median	Minimum	Maximum
2,000 or less	17.38%	17.50%	7.00%	31.00%
2,000 – 10,000	26.94%	24.50%	7.00%	80.00%
More than 10,000	35.91%	30.00%	10.00%	68.00%

Table 2.1.6 Percentage of personal computers that are Primarily for Staff of the Library Broken out by Total Annual Tuition

Total Annual Tuition	Mean	Median	Minimum	Maximum
Less than $5,000	22.08%	21.00%	10.00%	45.00%
$5,000 - $20,000	34.90%	27.50%	7.00%	68.00%
More than $20,000	27.42%	21.50%	7.00%	80.00%

Table 2.2.1 Percentage of personal computers that are Primarily for Library Patrons

	Mean	Median	Minimum	Maximum
Entire sample	72.11%	75.00%	20.00%	93.00%

Table 2.2.2 Percentage of personal computers that are Primarily for Library Patrons Broken out by Level of authority when making decisions about the purchase of new computer technologies

Level of authority when making decisions about the purchase of new computer technologies	Mean	Median	Minimum	Maximum
Recommend only	78.08%	79.00%	50.00%	93.00%
Need approval	70.64%	70.00%	20.00%	93.00%
Have authority to buy	66.55%	75.00%	32.00%	90.00%

Table 2.2.3 Percentage of personal computers that are Primarily for Library Patrons Broken out by Carnegie Class

Carnegie Class	Mean	Median	Minimum	Maximum
Community College	81.29%	86.00%	55.00%	93.00%
4-Year College	65.67%	72.50%	20.00%	90.00%
MA/PHD Granting Institution	74.00%	75.00%	50.00%	90.00%
Research University	50.40%	50.00%	32.00%	70.00%

Table 2.2.4 Percentage of personal computers that are Primarily for Library Patrons Broken out by Public Versus Private

Public Versus Private	Mean	Median	Minimum	Maximum
Public	73.54%	75.50%	32.00%	93.00%
Private	69.00%	75.00%	20.00%	90.00%

Table 2.2.5 Percentage of personal computers that are Primarily for Library Patrons Broken out by Total Annual Enrollment

Total Annual Enrollment	Mean	Median	Minimum	Maximum
2,000 or less	82.63%	82.50%	69.00%	93.00%
2,000 – 10,000	71.75%	75.00%	20.00%	93.00%
More than 10,000	65.00%	70.00%	32.00%	90.00%

Table 2.2.6 Percentage of personal computers that are Primarily for Library Patrons Broken out by Total Annual Tuition

Total Annual Tuition	Mean	Median	Minimum	Maximum
Less than $5,000	78.62%	79.00%	55.00%	90.00%
$5,000 - $20,000	65.10%	72.50%	32.00%	93.00%
More than $20,000	70.92%	74.00%	20.00%	93.00%

Table 3.1 How many personal computers or individual workstations did the library purchase in 2012?(once again the term personal computer for this report excludes laptops and tablets)

	Mean	Median	Minimum	Maximum
Entire sample	16.91	1.00	0.00	200.00

Table 3.2 How many personal computers or individual workstations did the library purchase in 2012?(once again the term personal computer for this report excludes laptops and tablets) Broken out by Level of authority when making decisions about the purchase of new computer technologies

Level of authority when making decisions about the purchase of new computer technologies	Mean	Median	Minimum	Maximum
Recommend only	0.54	0.00	0.00	5.00
Need approval	8.27	4.00	0.00	30.00
Have authority to buy	44.91	40.00	0.00	200.00

Table 3.3 How many personal computers or individual workstations did the library purchase in 2012?(once again the term personal computer for this report excludes laptops and tablets) Broken out by Carnegie Class

Carnegie Class	Mean	Median	Minimum	Maximum
Community College	2.29	0.00	0.00	28.00
4-Year College	4.83	4.00	0.00	13.00
MA/PHD Granting Institution	16.20	2.00	0.00	80.00
Research University	73.80	44.00	8.00	200.00

Table 3.4 How many personal computers or individual workstations did the library purchase in 2012?(once again the term personal computer for this report excludes laptops and tablets) Broken out by Public Versus Private

Public Versus Private	Mean	Median	Minimum	Maximum
Public	22.13	1.00	0.00	200.00
Private	5.55	3.00	0.00	30.00

Table 3.5 How many personal computers or individual workstations did the library purchase in 2012?(once again the term personal computer for this report excludes laptops and tablets) Broken out by Total Annual Enrollment

Total Annual Enrollment	Mean	Median	Minimum	Maximum
2,000 or less	4.38	1.00	0.00	28.00
2,000 – 10,000	4.25	0.00	0.00	30.00
More than 10,000	44.45	40.00	0.00	200.00

Table 3.6 How many personal computers or individual workstations did the library purchase in 2012?(once again the term personal computer for this report excludes laptops and tablets) Broken out by Total Annual Tuition

Total Annual Tuition	Mean	Median	Minimum	Maximum
Less than $5,000	0.92	0.00	0.00	8.00
$5,000 - $20,000	45.40	25.00	0.00	200.00
More than $20,000	10.50	4.50	0.00	40.00

Table 4.1 How many personal computers or workstations does the library plan to purchase in 2013?

	Mean	Median	Minimum	Maximum
Entire sample	21.12	2.00	0.00	200.00

Table 4.2 How many personal computers or workstations does the library plan to purchase in 2013? Broken out by Level of authority when making decisions about the purchase of new computer technologies

Level of authority when making decisions about the purchase of new computer technologies	Mean	Median	Minimum	Maximum
Recommend only	2.77	0.00	0.00	26.00
Need approval	10.70	11.50	0.00	30.00
Have authority to buy	52.27	40.00	0.00	200.00

Table 4.3 How many personal computers or workstations does the library plan to purchase in 2013? Broken out by Carnegie Class

Carnegie Class	Mean	Median	Minimum	Maximum
Community College	2.43	0.00	0.00	22.00
4-Year College	8.00	2.50	0.00	26.00
MA/PHD Granting Institution	20.56	8.00	0.00	80.00
Research University	90.20	48.00	13.00	200.00

Table 4.4 How many personal computers or workstations does the library plan to purchase in 2013? Broken out by Public Versus Private

Public Versus Private	Mean	Median	Minimum	Maximum
Public	25.79	1.00	0.00	200.00
Private	9.90	5.50	0.00	30.00

Table 4.5 How many personal computers or workstations does the library plan to purchase in 2013? Broken out by Total Annual Enrollment

Total Annual Enrollment	Mean	Median	Minimum	Maximum
2,000 or less	2.88	1.00	0.00	10.00
2,000 – 10,000	6.13	0.00	0.00	30.00
More than 10,000	54.82	40.00	0.00	200.00

Table 4.6 How many personal computers or workstations does the library plan to purchase in 2013? Broken out by Total Annual Tuition

Total Annual Tuition	Mean	Median	Minimum	Maximum
Less than $5,000	3.62	0.00	0.00	22.00
$5,000 - $20,000	53.30	24.00	0.00	200.00
More than $20,000	12.55	2.00	0.00	50.00

Table 5.1 Does the library's strategic technology plan call for "turning over' or replacing the library's stock of computers within a certain number of years?

	No Answer	Yes	No
Entire sample	0.00%	65.71%	34.29%

Table 5.2 Does the library's strategic technology plan call for "turning over' or replacing the library's stock of computers within a certain number of years? Broken out by Level of authority when making decisions about the purchase of new computer technologies

Level of authority when making decisions about the purchase of new computer technologies	Yes	No
Recommend only	38.46%	61.54%
Need approval	63.64%	36.36%
Have authority to buy	100.00%	0.00%

Table 5.3 Does the library's strategic technology plan call for "turning over' or replacing the library's stock of computers within a certain number of years? Broken out by Carnegie Class

Carnegie Class	Yes	No
Community College	50.00%	50.00%
4-Year College	83.33%	16.67%
MA/PHD Granting Institution	60.00%	40.00%
Research University	100.00%	0.00%

Table 5.4 Does the library's strategic technology plan call for "turning over' or replacing the library's stock of computers within a certain number of years? Broken out by Public Versus Private

Public Versus Private	Yes	No
Public	70.83%	29.17%
Private	54.55%	45.45%

Table 5.5 Does the library's strategic technology plan call for "turning over' or replacing the library's stock of computers within a certain number of years? Broken out by Total Annual Enrollment

Total Annual Enrollment	Yes	No
2,000 or less	62.50%	37.50%
2,000 – 10,000	56.25%	43.75%
More than 10,000	81.82%	18.18%

Table 5.6 Does the library's strategic technology plan call for "turning over' or replacing the library's stock of computers within a certain number of years? Broken out by Total Annual Tuition

Total Annual Tuition	Yes	No
Less than $5,000	53.85%	46.15%
$5,000 - $20,000	80.00%	20.00%
More than $20,000	66.67%	33.33%

Table 6.1 If so, how many years is this average "turn over" or replacement cycle for the personal computers used in the library as stipulated in plans and as actually practiced? Planned computer turn over cycle

	Mean	Median	Minimum	Maximum
Entire sample	3.78	3.00	3.00	5.00

Table 6.2 If so, how many years is this average "turn over" or replacement cycle for the personal computers used in the library as stipulated in plans and as actually practiced? Planned computer turn over cycle Broken out by Level of authority when making decisions about the purchase of new computer technologies

Level of authority when making decisions about the purchase of new computer technologies	Mean	Median	Minimum	Maximum
Recommend only	3.60	3.00	3.00	5.00
Need approval	3.71	3.00	3.00	5.00
Have authority to buy	3.91	4.00	3.00	5.00

Table 6.3 If so, how many years is this average "turn over" or replacement cycle for the personal computers used in the library as stipulated in plans and as actually practiced? Planned computer turn over cycle Broken out by Carnegie Class

Carnegie Class	Mean	Median	Minimum	Maximum
Community College	3.86	3.00	3.00	5.00
4-Year College	4.20	4.00	3.00	5.00
MA/PHD Granting Institution	3.67	3.50	3.00	5.00
Research University	3.40	3.00	3.00	5.00

Table 6.4 If so, how many years is this average "turn over" or replacement cycle for the personal computers used in the library as stipulated in plans and as actually practiced? Planned computer turn over cycle Broken out by Public Versus Private

Public Versus Private	Mean	Median	Minimum	Maximum
Public	3.71	3.00	3.00	5.00
Private	4.00	4.00	3.00	5.00

Table 6.5 If so, how many years is this average "turn over" or replacement cycle for the personal computers used in the library as stipulated in plans and as actually practiced? Planned computer turn over cycle Broken out by Total Annual Enrollment

Total Annual Enrollment	Mean	Median	Minimum	Maximum
2,000 or less	4.20	5.00	3.00	5.00
2,000 – 10,000	3.89	4.00	3.00	5.00
More than 10,000	3.44	3.00	3.00	5.00

Table 6.6 If so, how many years is this average "turn over" or replacement cycle for the personal computers used in the library as stipulated in plans and as actually practiced? Planned computer turn over cycle Broken out by Total Annual Tuition

Total Annual Tuition	Mean	Median	Minimum	Maximum
Less than $5,000	3.57	3.00	3.00	5.00
$5,000 - $20,000	3.88	3.50	3.00	5.00
More than $20,000	3.88	4.00	3.00	5.00

Table 7.1 If so, how many years is this average "turn over" or replacement cycle for the personal computers used in the library as stipulated in plans and as actually practiced? Actually practiced turn over cycle

	Mean	Median	Minimum	Maximum
Entire sample	4.68	5.00	3.00	9.00

Table 7.2 If so, how many years is this average "turn over" or replacement cycle for the personal computers used in the library as stipulated in plans and as actually practiced? Actually practiced turn over cycle Broken out by Level of authority when making decisions about the purchase of new computer technologies

Level of authority when making decisions about the purchase of new computer technologies	Mean	Median	Minimum	Maximum
Recommend only	3.50	3.50	3.00	4.00
Need approval	5.00	5.00	3.00	8.00
Have authority to buy	5.00	5.00	3.00	9.00

Table 7.3 If so, how many years is this average "turn over" or replacement cycle for the personal computers used in the library as stipulated in plans and as actually practiced? Actually practiced turn over cycle Broken out by Carnegie Class

Carnegie Class	Mean	Median	Minimum	Maximum
Community College	4.80	5.00	3.00	8.00
4-Year College	4.80	5.00	4.00	6.00
MA/PHD Granting Institution	3.50	3.00	3.00	5.00
Research University	5.40	5.00	4.00	9.00

Table 7.4 If so, how many years is this average "turn over" or replacement cycle for the personal computers used in the library as stipulated in plans and as actually practiced? Actually practiced turn over cycle Broken out by Public Versus Private

Public Versus Private	Mean	Median	Minimum	Maximum
Public	4.79	5.00	3.00	9.00
Private	4.40	4.00	3.00	6.00

Table 7.5 If so, how many years is this average "turn over" or replacement cycle for the personal computers used in the library as stipulated in plans and as actually practiced? Actually practiced turn over cycle Broken out by Total Annual Enrollment

Total Annual Enrollment	Mean	Median	Minimum	Maximum
2,000 or less	5.20	5.00	3.00	8.00
2,000 – 10,000	4.40	4.00	3.00	6.00
More than 10,000	4.56	4.00	3.00	9.00

Table 7.6 If so, how many years is this average "turn over" or replacement cycle for the personal computers used in the library as stipulated in plans and as actually practiced? Actually practiced turn over cycle Broken out by Total Annual Tuition

Total Annual Tuition	Mean	Median	Minimum	Maximum
Less than $5,000	4.20	5.00	3.00	5.00
$5,000 - $20,000	5.00	5.00	3.00	9.00
More than $20,000	4.71	4.00	3.00	8.00

Table 8 What percentage of the computers and workstations that the library plans to purchase in the next two years are:

Table 8.1.1 Percentage of computers and workstations the library plans to purchase that are made by Apple

	Mean	Median	Minimum	Maximum
Entire sample	3.70%	1.00%	0.00%	20.00%

Table 8.1.2 Percentage of computers and workstations the library plans to purchase that are made by Apple Broken out by Level of authority when making decisions about the purchase of new computer technologies

Level of authority when making decisions about the purchase of new computer technologies	Mean	Median	Minimum	Maximum
Recommend only	0.71%	0.00%	0.00%	5.00%
Need approval	4.43%	2.00%	0.00%	15.00%
Have authority to buy	5.44%	3.00%	0.00%	20.00%

Table 8.1.3 Percentage of computers and workstations the library plans to purchase that are made by Apple Broken out by Carnegie Class

Carnegie Class	Mean	Median	Minimum	Maximum
Community College	1.00%	0.00%	0.00%	8.00%
4-Year College	2.25%	2.00%	0.00%	5.00%
MA/PHD Granting Institution	5.43%	2.00%	0.00%	20.00%
Research University	7.50%	6.50%	2.00%	15.00%

Table 8.1.4 Percentage of computers and workstations the library plans to purchase that are made by Apple Broken out by Public Versus Private

Public Versus Private	Mean	Median	Minimum	Maximum
Public	4.50%	1.00%	0.00%	20.00%
Private	1.86%	1.00%	0.00%	5.00%

Table 8.1.5 Percentage of computers and workstations the library plans to purchase that are made by Apple Broken out by Total Annual Enrollment

Total Annual Enrollment	Mean	Median	Minimum	Maximum
2,000 or less	1.33%	0.00%	0.00%	8.00%
2,000 – 10,000	2.13%	1.50%	0.00%	5.00%
More than 10,000	6.67%	3.00%	0.00%	20.00%

Table 8.1.6 Percentage of computers and workstations the library plans to purchase that are made by Apple Broken out by Total Annual Tuition

Total Annual Tuition	Mean	Median	Minimum	Maximum
Less than $5,000	1.88%	0.00%	0.00%	15.00%
$5,000 - $20,000	5.57%	3.00%	0.00%	20.00%
More than $20,000	3.88%	3.50%	0.00%	10.00%

Table 8.2.1 Percentage of computers and workstations the library plans to purchase that are made by IBM or IBM clones that use Windows/Vista operating system

	Mean	Median	Minimum	Maximum
Entire sample	75.38%	98.00%	0.00%	112.00%

Table 8.2.2 Percentage of computers and workstations the library plans to purchase that are made by IBM or IBM clones that use Windows/Vista operating system Broken out by Level of authority when making decisions about the purchase of new computer technologies

Level of authority when making decisions about the purchase of new computer technologies	Mean	Median	Minimum	Maximum
Recommend only	58.00%	100.00%	0.00%	112.00%
Need approval	68.22%	95.00%	0.00%	100.00%
Have authority to buy	95.45%	98.00%	79.00%	100.00%

Table 8.2.3 Percentage of computers and workstations the library plans to purchase that are made by IBM or IBM clones that use Windows/Vista operating system Broken out by Carnegie Class

Carnegie Class	Mean	Median	Minimum	Maximum
Community College	58.55%	100.00%	0.00%	112.00%
4-Year College	62.20%	96.00%	0.00%	100.00%
MA/PHD Granting Institution	95.13%	98.50%	79.00%	100.00%
Research University	94.00%	97.00%	85.00%	100.00%

Table 8.2.4 Percentage of computers and workstations the library plans to purchase that are made by IBM or IBM clones that use Windows/Vista operating system Broken out by Public Versus Private

Public Versus Private	Mean	Median	Minimum	Maximum
Public	75.19%	97.00%	0.00%	112.00%
Private	75.88%	98.50%	0.00%	100.00%

Table 8.2.5 Percentage of computers and workstations the library plans to purchase that are made by IBM or IBM clones that use Windows/Vista operating system Broken out by Total Annual Enrollment

Total Annual Enrollment	Mean	Median	Minimum	Maximum
2,000 or less	72.86%	100.00%	0.00%	100.00%
2,000 – 10,000	76.25%	98.50%	0.00%	112.00%
More than 10,000	76.10%	90.00%	0.00%	100.00%

Table 8.2.6 Percentage of computers and workstations the library plans to purchase that are made by IBM or IBM clones that use Windows/Vista operating system Broken out by Total Annual Tuition

Total Annual Tuition	Mean	Median	Minimum	Maximum
Less than $5,000	62.90%	92.50%	0.00%	112.00%
$5,000 - $20,000	96.00%	99.00%	79.00%	100.00%
More than $20,000	66.33%	95.00%	0.00%	100.00%

Table 8.3.1 Percentage of computers and workstations the library plans to purchase that are made by Other

	Mean	Median	Minimum	Maximum
Entire sample	8.29%	0.00%	0.00%	95.00%

Table 8.3.2 Percentage of computers and workstations the library plans to purchase that are made by Other Broken out by Level of authority when making decisions about the purchase of new computer technologies

Level of authority when making decisions about the purchase of new computer technologies	Mean	Median	Minimum	Maximum
Recommend only	13.57%	0.00%	0.00%	95.00%
Need approval	6.67%	0.00%	0.00%	20.00%
Have authority to buy	0.25%	0.00%	0.00%	1.00%

Table 8.3.3 Percentage of computers and workstations the library plans to purchase that are made by Other Broken out by Carnegie Class

Carnegie Class	Mean	Median	Minimum	Maximum
Community College	3.33%	0.00%	0.00%	20.00%
4-Year College	31.67%	0.00%	0.00%	95.00%
MA/PHD Granting Institution	0.25%	0.00%	0.00%	1.00%
Research University	0.00%	0.00%	0.00%	0.00%

Table 8.3.4 Percentage of computers and workstations the library plans to purchase that are made by Other Broken out by Public Versus Private

Public Versus Private	Mean	Median	Minimum	Maximum
Public	2.10%	0.00%	0.00%	20.00%
Private	23.75%	0.00%	0.00%	95.00%

Table 8.3.5 Percentage of computers and workstations the library plans to purchase that are made by Other Broken out by Total Annual Enrollment

Total Annual Enrollment	Mean	Median	Minimum	Maximum
2,000 or less	4.00%	0.00%	0.00%	20.00%
2,000 – 10,000	19.00%	0.00%	0.00%	95.00%
More than 10,000	0.25%	0.00%	0.00%	1.00%

Table 8.3.6 Percentage of computers and workstations the library plans to purchase that are made by Other Broken out by Total Annual Tuition

Total Annual Tuition	Mean	Median	Minimum	Maximum
Less than $5,000	0.00%	0.00%	0.00%	0.00%
$5,000 - $20,000	0.25%	0.00%	0.00%	1.00%
More than $20,000	23.00%	0.00%	0.00%	95.00%

Table 9.1 Approximately how much did the library spend for personal computers and workstations in the past year, the 2012-13 academic year?

	Mean	Median	Minimum	Maximum
Entire sample	$17,193.33	$950.00	$0.00	$175,000.00

Table 9.2 Approximately how much did the library spend for personal computers and workstations in the past year, the 2012-13 academic year? Broken out by Level of authority when making decisions about the purchase of new computer technologies

Level of authority when making decisions about the purchase of new computer technologies	Mean	Median	Minimum	Maximum
Recommend only	$3,263.64	$0.00	$0.00	$34,000.00
Need approval	$6,600.00	$2,000.00	$0.00	$24,000.00
Have authority to buy	$38,827.27	$16,000.00	$0.00	$175,000.00

Table 9.3 Approximately how much did the library spend for personal computers and workstations in the past year, the 2012-13 academic year? Broken out by Carnegie Class

Carnegie Class	Mean	Median	Minimum	Maximum
Community College	$5,233.33	$0.00	$0.00	$34,000.00
4-Year College	$3,000.00	$1,000.00	$0.00	$10,000.00
MA/PHD Granting Institution	$5,262.50	$450.00	$0.00	$20,000.00
Research University	$79,180.00	$43,000.00	$14,000.00	$175,000.00

Table 9.4 Approximately how much did the library spend for personal computers and workstations in the past year, the 2012-13 academic year? Broken out by Public Versus Private

Public Versus Private	Mean	Median	Minimum	Maximum
Public	$22,722.73	$2,000.00	$0.00	$175,000.00
Private	$1,987.50	$450.00	$0.00	$10,000.00

Table 9.5 Approximately how much did the library spend for personal computers and workstations in the past year, the 2012-13 academic year? Broken out by Total Annual Enrollment

Total Annual Enrollment	Mean	Median	Minimum	Maximum
2,000 or less	$4,100.00	$900.00	$0.00	$24,000.00
2,000 – 10,000	$1,425.00	$0.00	$0.00	$10,000.00
More than 10,000	$46,590.00	$27,000.00	$0.00	$175,000.00

Table 9.6 Approximately how much did the library spend for personal computers and workstations in the past year, the 2012-13 academic year? Broken out by Total Annual Tuition

Total Annual Tuition	Mean	Median	Minimum	Maximum
Less than $5,000	$4,400.00	$0.00	$0.00	$34,000.00
$5,000 - $20,000	$45,233.33	$16,000.00	$0.00	$175,000.00
More than $20,000	$6,211.11	$900.00	$0.00	$24,000.00

Table 10.1 How much does the library (or the college in its name) plan to spend on personal computers in the upcoming 2013-14 academic year?

	Mean	Median	Minimum	Maximum
Entire sample	$26,206.32	$5,750.00	$0.00	$200,000.00

Table 10.2 How much does the library (or the college in its name) plan to spend on personal computers in the upcoming 2013-14 academic year? Broken out by Level of authority when making decisions about the purchase of new computer technologies

Level of authority when making decisions about the purchase of new computer technologies	Mean	Median	Minimum	Maximum
Recommend only	$15,363.64	$0.00	$0.00	$110,000.00
Need approval	$6,434.63	$7,750.00	$0.00	$14,000.00
Have authority to buy	$57,033.33	$20,000.00	$0.00	$200,000.00

Table 10.3 How much does the library (or the college in its name) plan to spend on personal computers in the upcoming 2013-14 academic year? Broken out by Carnegie Class

Carnegie Class	Mean	Median	Minimum	Maximum
Community College	$11,836.36	$0.00	$0.00	$110,000.00
4-Year College	$3,694.25	$2,250.00	$0.00	$10,277.00
MA/PHD Granting Institution	$12,850.00	$7,750.00	$0.00	$50,000.00
Research University	$97,200.00	$50,000.00	$14,000.00	$200,000.00

Table 10.4 How much does the library (or the college in its name) plan to spend on personal computers in the upcoming 2013-14 academic year? Broken out by Public Versus Private

Public Versus Private	Mean	Median	Minimum	Maximum
Public	$35,175.00	$9,000.00	$0.00	$200,000.00
Private	$3,784.63	$2,250.00	$0.00	$1,0277.00

Table 10.5 How much does the library (or the college in its name) plan to spend on personal computers in the upcoming 2013-14 academic year? Broken out by Total Annual Enrollment

Total Annual Enrollment	Mean	Median	Minimum	Maximum
2,000 or less	$4,428.57	$4,000.00	$0.00	$10,000.00
2,000 – 10,000	$1,888.82	$0.00	$0.00	$10,277.00
More than 10,000	$68,200.00	$48,500.00	$0.00	$200,000.00

Table 10.6 How much does the library (or the college in its name) plan to spend on personal computers in the upcoming 2013-14 academic year? Broken out by Total Annual Tuition

Total Annual Tuition	Mean	Median	Minimum	Maximum
Less than $5,000	$12,200.00	$0.00	$0.00	$110,000.00
$5,000 - $20,000	$62,662.50	$31,500.00	$1,300.00	$200,000.00
More than $20,000	$10,919.67	$7,500.00	$0.00	$50,000.00

Table 10.7 Which brands of laptop has your library preferred in recent years and why?

1. Lenovo, ThinkPads, because that's what campus IT recommended.
2. Lenovo, State contract.
3. HP - best price.
4. Toshiba.
5. Dell - service/support/price.
6. HP - supported by campus; expanding emphasis on MacAir.
7. HP.
8. HP - this what IT decided.
9. Dell - quality and service plan.
10. Tough books. Low bid.
11. Dell.
12. HP - college standard, Apple - college standard.
13. Dell - we have no say in the choice of brand.
14. Dell - university contract.
15. Dell because of a discount.
16. Dell - IT decision.
17. Dell. We aren't really given an option. Our institutional IT people decide.
18. Dell (due to state contract) and Macs.
19. Dell - solid machines, supported by our campus IT, good price. Apple - expensive, but a few people prefer them, they hold up well, and can dual-boot into Windows.
20. Dell - reliable and available via state-wide educational pricing contract; Toshiba - reliable. MSI netbooks not found to be rugged enough.
21. We have no choice in brands.
22. HP - College IT dept. has discount with HP.
23. Dell - State purchasing list. Discounts from them.
24. Lenovo - IT determined them; vendor of choice.
25. Dell. That is what our IT orders.
26. Dell, again because we have a contract with them
27. Our IT dept. purchases HP laptops, but other than 14 public laptops in an electronic classroom, we do not provide or purchase laptops.
28. Dell - Service consideration. Macs.
29. Dell - low bid.
30. Toshiba - these are on state bid.
31. No particular brand.
32. HP, but these laptops were not purchased recently. I do not know how the decision was made. I strongly suspect it had to do with the college's purchasing policy.
33. We purchased a Dell on the advice of the campus IT department.

Table 11.1 How many laptop computers did the library purchase in the past year?

	Mean	Median	Minimum	Maximum
Entire sample	5.12	0.00	0.00	41.00

Table 11.2 How many laptop computers did the library purchase in the past year? Broken out by Level of authority when making decisions about the purchase of new computer technologies

Level of authority when making decisions about the purchase of new computer technologies	Mean	Median	Minimum	Maximum
Recommend only	2.17	0.00	0.00	25.00
Need approval	2.27	0.00	0.00	21.00
Have authority to buy	11.18	4.00	0.00	41.00

Table 11.3 How many laptop computers did the library purchase in the past year? Broken out by Carnegie Class

Carnegie Class	Mean	Median	Minimum	Maximum
Community College	2.14	0.00	0.00	25.00
4-Year College	1.60	0.00	0.00	6.00
MA/PHD Granting Institution	3.30	0.00	0.00	21.00
Research University	20.60	25.00	2.00	41.00

Table 11.4 How many laptop computers did the library purchase in the past year? Broken out by Public Versus Private

Public Versus Private	Mean	Median	Minimum	Maximum
Public	6.29	0.00	0.00	41.00
Private	2.30	0.00	0.00	21.00

Table 11.5 How many laptop computers did the library purchase in the past year? Broken out by Total Annual Enrollment

Total Annual Enrollment	Mean	Median	Minimum	Maximum
2,000 or less	0.50	0.00	0.00	4.00
2,000 – 10,000	1.93	0.00	0.00	21.00
More than 10,000	12.82	2.00	0.00	41.00

Table 11.6 How many laptop computers did the library purchase in the past year? Broken out by Total Annual Tuition

Total Annual Tuition	Mean	Median	Minimum	Maximum
Less than $5,000	2.46	0.00	0.00	25.00
$5,000 - $20,000	11.70	4.00	0.00	41.00
More than $20,000	2.27	0.00	0.00	21.00

Table 12.1 What is the library's total stock of laptop computers including those for librarians and other personnel as well as for patrons?

	Mean	Median	Minimum	Maximum
Entire sample	38.21	19.00	0.00	275.00

Table 12.2 What is the library's total stock of laptop computers including those for librarians and other personnel as well as for patrons? Broken out by Level of authority when making decisions about the purchase of new computer technologies

Level of authority when making decisions about the purchase of new computer technologies	Mean	Median	Minimum	Maximum
Recommend only	33.17	18.50	0.00	150.00
Need approval	10.55	7.00	0.00	25.00
Have authority to buy	71.36	36.00	1.00	275.00

Table 12.3 What is the library's total stock of laptop computers including those for librarians and other personnel as well as for patrons? Broken out by Carnegie Class

Carnegie Class	Mean	Median	Minimum	Maximum
Community College	25.62	8.00	0.00	150.00
4-Year College	16.33	6.00	1.00	60.00
MA/PHD Granting Institution	39.90	23.00	2.00	191.00
Research University	93.80	64.00	20.00	275.00

Table 12.4 What is the library's total stock of laptop computers including those for librarians and other personnel as well as for patrons? Broken out by Public Versus Private

Public Versus Private	Mean	Median	Minimum	Maximum
Public	49.61	22.00	0.00	275.00
Private	14.36	7.00	1.00	60.00

Table 12.5 What is the library's total stock of laptop computers including those for librarians and other personnel as well as for patrons? Broken out by Total Annual Enrollment

Total Annual Enrollment	Mean	Median	Minimum	Maximum
2,000 or less	3.00	2.00	0.00	8.00
2,000 - 10,000	28.13	19.50	2.00	150.00
More than 10,000	82.50	57.00	0.00	275.00

Table 12.6 What is the library's total stock of laptop computers including those for librarians and other personnel as well as for patrons? Broken out by Total Annual Tuition

Total Annual Tuition	Mean	Median	Minimum	Maximum
Less than $5,000	17.33	11.50	0.00	75.00
$5,000 - $20,000	70.50	43.00	1.00	275.00
More than $20,000	32.17	16.00	0.00	191.00

Table 13 Of the total number of laptops how many are for library patrons and how many for staff?

Table 13.1.1 Number of laptops reserved for library patrons

	Mean	Median	Minimum	Maximum
Entire sample	32.64	16.00	0.00	225.00

Table 13.1.2 Number of laptops reserved for library patrons Broken out by Level of authority when making decisions about the purchase of new computer technologies

Level of authority when making decisions about the purchase of new computer technologies	Mean	Median	Minimum	Maximum
Recommend only	28.33	10.50	0.00	150.00
Need approval	10.10	9.50	0.00	21.00
Have authority to buy	57.82	30.00	0.00	225.00

Table 13.1.3 Number of laptops reserved for library patrons Broken out by Carnegie Class

Carnegie Class	Mean	Median	Minimum	Maximum
Community College	25.50	7.50	0.00	150.00
4-Year College	11.33	2.50	0.00	43.00
MA/PHD Granting Institution	34.70	18.50	0.00	185.00
Research University	71.20	41.00	0.00	225.00

Table 13.1.4 Number of laptops reserved for library patrons Broken out by Public Versus Private

Public Versus Private	Mean	Median	Minimum	Maximum
Public	43.86	19.50	0.00	225.00
Private	10.18	4.00	0.00	43.00

Table 13.1.5 Number of laptops reserved for library patrons Broken out by Total Annual Enrollment

Total Annual Enrollment	Mean	Median	Minimum	Maximum
2,000 or less	2.00	0.50	0.00	6.00
2,000 - 10,000	23.88	16.00	0.00	150.00
More than 10,000	75.44	41.00	0.00	225.00

Table 13.1.6 Number of laptops reserved for library patrons Broken out by Total Annual Tuition

Total Annual Tuition	Mean	Median	Minimum	Maximum
Less than $5,000	16.00	9.00	0.00	68.00
$5,000 - $20,000	56.50	29.50	0.00	225.00
More than $20,000	28.00	13.00	0.00	185.00

Table 13.2.1 Number of laptops reserved for library staff

	Mean	Median	Minimum	Maximum
Entire sample	6.76	3.00	0.00	50.00

Table 13.2.2 Number of laptops reserved for library staff Broken out by Level of authority when making decisions about the purchase of new computer technologies

Level of authority when making decisions about the purchase of new computer technologies	Mean	Median	Minimum	Maximum
Recommend only	4.83	3.00	0.00	17.00
Need approval	1.50	1.50	0.00	5.00
Have authority to buy	13.64	7.00	1.00	50.00

Table 13.2.3 Number of laptops reserved for library staff Broken out by Carnegie Class

Carnegie Class	Mean	Median	Minimum	Maximum
Community College	2.25	2.00	0.00	7.00
4-Year College	5.17	3.00	1.00	17.00
MA/PHD Granting Institution	5.20	2.00	0.00	20.00
Research University	22.60	20.00	5.00	50.00

Table 13.2.4 Number of laptops reserved for library staff Broken out by Public Versus Private

Public Versus Private	Mean	Median	Minimum	Maximum
Public	8.00	3.50	0.00	50.00
Private	4.27	2.00	0.00	17.00

Table 13.2.5 Number of laptops reserved for library staff Broken out by Total Annual Enrollment

Total Annual Enrollment	Mean	Median	Minimum	Maximum
2,000 or less	1.13	1.50	0.00	2.00
2,000 – 10,000	4.25	3.00	0.00	17.00
More than 10,000	16.22	15.00	0.00	50.00

Table 13.2.6 Number of laptops reserved for library staff Broken out by Total Annual Tuition

Total Annual Tuition	Mean	Median	Minimum	Maximum
Less than $5,000	2.91	2.00	0.00	7.00
$5,000 - $20,000	14.10	11.00	0.00	50.00
More than $20,000	4.17	2.00	0.00	17.00

Table 14.1 If you have had losses due to theft of laptops or other mobile computing devices what is the total replacement cost for the items lost (even if you did Not replace them)

	Mean	Median	Minimum	Maximum
Entire sample	$1,058.82	$500.00	$0.00	$6,000.00

Table 14.2 If you have had losses due to theft of laptops or other mobile computing devices what is the total replacement cost for the items lost (even if you did Not replace them) Broken out by Level of authority when making decisions about the purchase of new computer technologies

Level of authority when making decisions about the purchase of new computer technologies	Mean	Median	Minimum	Maximum
Recommend only	$500.00	$0.00	$0.00	$1,800.00
Need approval	$200.00	$0.00	$0.00	$600.00
Have authority to buy	$2,580.00	$2,400.00	$0.00	$6,000.00

Table 14.3 If you have had losses due to theft of laptops or other mobile computing devices what is the total replacement cost for the items lost (even if you did Not replace them) Broken out by Carnegie Class

Carnegie Class	Mean	Median	Minimum	Maximum
Community College	$562.50	$250.00	$0.00	$1,800.00
4-Year College	$1,500.00	$1,500.00	$0.00	$3,000.00
MA/PHD Granting Institution	$2,100.00	$1,200.00	$0.00	$6,000.00
Research University	$300.00	$300.00	$0.00	$600.00

Table 14.4 If you have had losses due to theft of laptops or other mobile computing devices what is the total replacement cost for the items lost (even if you did Not replace them) Broken out by Public Versus Private

Public Versus Private	Mean	Median	Minimum	Maximum
Public	$1,071.43	$550.00	$0.00	$6,000.00
Private	$1,000.00	$0.00	$0.00	$3,000.00

Table 14.5 If you have had losses due to theft of laptops or other mobile computing devices what is the total replacement cost for the items lost (even if you did Not replace them) Broken out by Total Annual Enrollment

Total Annual Enrollment	Mean	Median	Minimum	Maximum
2,000 or less	$700.00	$0.00	$0.00	$3,000.00
2,000 – 10,000	$440.00	$0.00	$0.00	$1,500.00
More than 10,000	$1,757.14	$1,500.00	$0.00	$6,000.00

Table 14.6 If you have had losses due to theft of laptops or other mobile computing devices what is the total replacement cost for the items lost (even if you did Not replace them) Broken out by Total Annual Tuition

Total Annual Tuition	Mean	Median	Minimum	Maximum
Less than $5,000	$628.57	$500.00	$0.00	$1,800.00
$5,000 - $20,000	$1,520.00	$1,500.00	$0.00	$3,000.00
More than $20,000	$1,200.00	$0.00	$0.00	$6,000.00

Table 15 How much did the library spend in the past year (the 2012-13 academic year) on the following types of technology?

Table 15.1.1 Amount spent on laptops in 2012-13

	Mean	Median	Minimum	Maximum
Entire sample	$4,863.64	$0.00	$0.00	$65,000.00

Table 15.1.2 Amount spent on laptops in 2012-13 Broken out by Level of authority when making decisions about the purchase of new computer technologies

Level of authority when making decisions about the purchase of new computer technologies	Mean	Median	Minimum	Maximum
Recommend only	$1,941.67	$0.00	$0.00	$22,000.00
Need approval	$1,490.00	$0.00	$0.00	$12,600.00
Have authority to buy	$11,118.18	$3,000.00	$0.00	$65,000.00

Table 15.1.3 Amount spent on laptops in 2012-13 Broken out by Carnegie Class

Carnegie Class	Mean	Median	Minimum	Maximum
Community College	$1,971.43	$0.00	$0.00	$22,000.00
4-Year College	$60.00	$0.00	$0.00	$300.00
MA/PHD Granting Institution	$3,177.78	$0.00	$0.00	$12,600.00
Research University	$20,800.00	$3,000.00	$0.00	$65,000.00

Table 15.1.4 Amount spent on laptops in 2012-13 Broken out by Public Versus Private

Public Versus Private	Mean	Median	Minimum	Maximum
Public	$6,150.00	$0.00	$0.00	$65,000.00
Private	$1,433.33	$0.00	$0.00	$12,600.00

Table 15.1.5 Amount spent on laptops in 2012-13 Broken out by Total Annual Enrollment

Total Annual Enrollment	Mean	Median	Minimum	Maximum
2,000 or less	$537.50	$0.00	$0.00	$4,300.00
2,000 – 10,000	$921.43	$0.00	$0.00	$12,600.00
More than 10,000	$13,027.27	$3,000.00	$0.00	$65,000.00

Table 15.1.6 Amount spent on laptops in 2012-13 Broken out by Total Annual Tuition

Total Annual Tuition	Mean	Median	Minimum	Maximum
Less than $5,000	$2,276.92	$0.00	$0.00	$22,000.00
$5,000 - $20,000	$11,400.00	$0.00	$0.00	$65,000.00
More than $20,000	$1,690.00	$0.00	$0.00	$12,600.00

Table 15.2.1 Amount spent on tablet computers in 2012-13

	Mean	Median	Minimum	Maximum
Entire sample	$1,039.12	$0.00	$0.00	$15,000.00

Table 15.2.2 Amount spent on tablet computers in 2012-13 Broken out by Level of authority when making decisions about the purchase of new computer technologies

Level of authority when making decisions about the purchase of new computer technologies	Mean	Median	Minimum	Maximum
Recommend only	$563.85	$0.00	$0.00	$4,180.00
Need approval	$340.00	$0.00	$0.00	$2,000.00
Have authority to buy	$2,236.36	$200.00	$0.00	$15,000.00

Table 15.2.3 Amount spent on tablet computers in 2012-13 Broken out by Carnegie Class

Carnegie Class	Mean	Median	Minimum	Maximum
Community College	$416.43	$0.00	$0.00	$4,180.00
4-Year College	$0.00	$0.00	$0.00	$0.00
MA/PHD Granting Institution	$1,466.67	$1,000.00	$0.00	$5,000.00
Research University	$3,260.00	$500.00	$0.00	$15,000.00

Table 15.2.4 Amount spent on tablet computers in 2012-13 Broken out by Public Versus Private

Public Versus Private	Mean	Median	Minimum	Maximum
Public	$1,288.75	$0.00	$0.00	$15,000.00
Private	$440.00	$0.00	$0.00	$2,400.00

Table 15.2.5 Amount spent on tablet computers in 2012-13Broken out by Total Annual Enrollment

Total Annual Enrollment	Mean	Median	Minimum	Maximum
2,000 or less	$168.75	$0.00	$0.00	$750.00
2,000 - 10,000	$500.00	$0.00	$0.00	$2,800.00
More than 10,000	$2,407.27	$500.00	$0.00	$15,000.00

Table 15.2.6 Amount spent on tablet computers in 2012-13Broken out by Total Annual Tuition

Total Annual Tuition	Mean	Median	Minimum	Maximum
Less than $5,000	$486.92	$0.00	$0.00	$4,180.00
$5,000 - $20,000	$2,360.00	$100.00	$0.00	$15,000.00
More than $20,000	$490.91	$0.00	$0.00	$2,400.00

Table 15.3.1 Amount spent on Netbooks in 2012-13

	Mean	Median	Minimum	Maximum
Entire sample	$0.00	$0.00	$0.00	$0.00

Table 15.3.2 Amount spent on Netbooks in 2012-13 Broken out by Level of authority when making decisions about the purchase of new computer technologies

Level of authority when making decisions about the purchase of new computer technologies	Mean	Median	Minimum	Maximum
Recommend only	$0.00	$0.00	$0.00	$0.00
Need approval	$0.00	$0.00	$0.00	$0.00
Have authority to buy	$0.00	$0.00	$0.00	$0.00

Table 15.3.3 Amount spent on Netbooks in 2012-13 Broken out by Carnegie Class

Carnegie Class	Mean	Median	Minimum	Maximum
Community College	$0.00	$0.00	$0.00	$0.00
4-Year College	$0.00	$0.00	$0.00	$0.00
MA/PHD Granting Institution	$0.00	$0.00	$0.00	$0.00
Research University	$0.00	$0.00	$0.00	$0.00

Table 15.3.4 Amount spent on Netbooks in 2012-13 Broken out by Public Versus Private

Public Versus Private	Mean	Median	Minimum	Maximum
Public	$0.00	$0.00	$0.00	$0.00
Private	$0.00	$0.00	$0.00	$0.00

Table 15.3.5 Amount spent on Netbooks in 2012-13 Broken out by Total Annual Enrollment

Total Annual Enrollment	Mean	Median	Minimum	Maximum
2,000 or less	$0.00	$0.00	$0.00	$0.00
2,000 – 10,000	$0.00	$0.00	$0.00	$0.00
More than 10,000	$0.00	$0.00	$0.00	$0.00

Table 15.3.6 Amount spent on Netbooks in 2012-13 Broken out by Total Annual Tuition

Total Annual Tuition	Mean	Median	Minimum	Maximum
Less than $5,000	$0.00	$0.00	$0.00	$0.00
$5,000 - $20,000	$0.00	$0.00	$0.00	$0.00
More than $20,000	$0.00	$0.00	$0.00	$0.00

Table 16 How much will the library spend in the next year, the 2013-14 academic year, on the following types of technology?

Table 16.1.1 Anticipated spending on laptops for 2013-14

	Mean	Median	Minimum	Maximum
Entire sample	$18,927.23	$0.00	$0.00	$275,000.00

Table 16.1.2 Anticipated spending on laptops for 2013-14 Broken out by Level of authority when making decisions about the purchase of new computer technologies

Level of authority when making decisions about the purchase of new computer technologies	Mean	Median	Minimum	Maximum
Recommend only	$27,291.67	$0.00	$0.00	$275,000.00
Need approval	$2,679.67	$0.00	$0.00	$12,517.00
Have authority to buy	$24,022.22	$2,200.00	$0.00	$200,000.00

Table 16.1.3 Anticipated spending on laptops for 2013-14 Broken out by Carnegie Class

Carnegie Class	Mean	Median	Minimum	Maximum
Community College	$19,835.71	$0.00	$0.00	$275,000.00
4-Year College	$4,629.25	$3,000.00	$0.00	$12,517.00
MA/PHD Granting Institution	$8,800.00	$0.00	$0.00	$50,000.00
Research University	$42,000.00	$3,000.00	$0.00	$200,000.00

Table 16.1.4 Anticipated spending on laptops for 2013-14 Broken out by Public Versus Private

Public Versus Private	Mean	Median	Minimum	Maximum
Public	$24,440.91	$0.00	$0.00	$275,000.00
Private	$3,764.63	$1000.00	$0.00	$12,517.00

Table 16.1.5 Anticipated spending on laptops for 2013-14 Broken out by Total Annual Enrollment

Total Annual Enrollment	Mean	Median	Minimum	Maximum
2,000 or less	$1,337.50	$250.00	$0.00	$6,000.00
2,000 – 10,000	$1,701.31	$0.00	$0.00	$12,517.00
More than 10,000	$59,444.44	$3,000.00	$0.00	$275,000.00

Table 16.1.6 Anticipated spending on laptops for 2013-14 Broken out by Total Annual Tuition

Total Annual Tuition	Mean	Median	Minimum	Maximum
Less than $5,000	$21,515.38	$0.00	0.00	275000.00
$5,000 - $20,000	$24,000.00	$2,000.00	$0.00	$200,000.00
More than $20,000	$9,014.63	$0.00	$0.00	$50,000.00

Table 16.2.1 Anticipated spending on Tablet Computers for 2013-14

	Mean	Median	Minimum	Maximum
Entire sample	$1,552.57	$0.00	$0.00	$25,000.00

Table 16.2.2 Anticipated spending on Tablet Computers for 2013-14 Broken out by Level of authority when making decisions about the purchase of new computer technologies

Level of authority when making decisions about the purchase of new computer technologies	Mean	Median	Minimum	Maximum
Recommend only	$308.33	$0.00	$0.00	$3,200.00
Need approval	$1,619.67	$0.00	$0.00	$10,277.00
Have authority to buy	$3,144.44	$0.00	$0.00	$25,000.00

Table 16.2.3 Anticipated spending on Tablet Computers for 2013-14 Broken out by Carnegie Class

Carnegie Class	Mean	Median	Minimum	Maximum
Community College	$138.46	$0.00	$0.00	$800.00
4-Year College	$2,695.40	$0.00	$0.00	$10,277.00
MA/PHD Granting Institution	$285.71	$0.00	$0.00	$2,000.00
Research University	$5,860.00	$1,500.00	$0.00	$25,000.00

Table 16.2.4 Anticipated spending on Tablet Computers for 2013-14 Broken out by Public Versus Private

Public Versus Private	Mean	Median	Minimum	Maximum
Public	$1,480.95	$0.00	$0.00	$25,000.00
Private	$1,719.67	$0.00	$0.00	$10,277.00

Table 16.2.5 Anticipated spending on Tablet Computers Broken out by Total Annual Enrollment

Total Annual Enrollment	Mean	Median	Minimum	Maximum
2,000 or less	$125.00	$0.00	$0.00	$500.00
2,000 – 10,000	$1,190.54	$0.00	$0.00	$10,277.00
More than 10,000	$3,344.44	$0.00	$0.00	$25,000.00

Table 16.2.6 Anticipated spending on Tablet Computers for 2013-14 Broken out by Total Annual Tuition

Total Annual Tuition	Mean	Median	Minimum	Maximum
Less than $5,000	$275.00	$0.00	$0.00	$1,500.00
$5,000 - $20,000	$3,088.89	$0.00	$0.00	$25,000.00
More than $20,000	$1,719.67	$0.00	$0.00	$10,277.00

Table 16.3.1 Anticipated spending on Netbooks for 2013-14

	Mean	Median	Minimum	Maximum
Entire sample	$0.00	$0.00	$0.00	$0.00

Table 16.3.2 Anticipated spending on Netbooks for 2013-14 Broken out by Level of authority when making decisions about the purchase of new computer technologies

Level of authority when making decisions about the purchase of new computer technologies	Mean	Median	Minimum	Maximum
Recommend only	$0.00	$0.00	$0.00	$0.00
Need approval	$0.00	$0.00	$0.00	$0.00
Have authority to buy	$0.00	$0.00	$0.00	$0.00

Table 16.3.3 Anticipated spending on Netbooks for 2013-14 Broken out by Carnegie Class

Carnegie Class	Mean	Median	Minimum	Maximum
Community College	$0.00	$0.00	$0.00	$0.00
4-Year College	$0.00	$0.00	$0.00	$0.00
MA/PHD Granting Institution	$0.00	$0.00	$0.00	$0.00
Research University	$0.00	$0.00	$0.00	$0.00

Table 16.3.4 Anticipated spending on Netbooks for 2013-14 Broken out by Public Versus Private

Public Versus Private	Mean	Median	Minimum	Maximum
Public	$0.00	$0.00	$0.00	$0.00
Private	$0.00	$0.00	$0.00	$0.00

Table 16.3.5 Anticipated spending on Netbooks for 2013-14 Broken out by Total Annual Enrollment

Total Annual Enrollment	Mean	Median	Minimum	Maximum
2,000 or less	$0.00	$0.00	$0.00	$0.00
2,000 - 10,000	$0.00	$0.00	$0.00	$0.00
More than 10,000	$0.00	$0.00	$0.00	$0.00

Table 16.3.6 Anticipated spending on Netbooks for 2013-14 Broken out by Total Annual Tuition

Total Annual Tuition	Mean	Median	Minimum	Maximum
Less than $5,000	$0.00	$0.00	$0.00	$0.00
$5,000 - $20,000	$0.00	$0.00	$0.00	$0.00
More than $20,000	$0.00	$0.00	$0.00	$0.00

Table 17.1 How many computers does the library have that can dual boot Apple and Microsoft operating systems?

	Mean	Median	Minimum	Maximum
Entire sample	3.86	0.00	0.00	56.00

Table 17.2 How many computers does the library have that can dual boot Apple and Microsoft operating systems? Broken out by Level of authority when making decisions about the purchase of new computer technologies

Level of authority when making decisions about the purchase of new computer technologies	Mean	Median	Minimum	Maximum
Recommend only	0.62	0.00	0.00	8.00
Need approval	2.45	0.00	0.00	15.00
Have authority to buy	9.09	1.00	0.00	56.00

Table 17.3 How many computers does the library have that can dual boot Apple and Microsoft operating systems? Broken out by Carnegie Class

Carnegie Class	Mean	Median	Minimum	Maximum
Community College	1.14	0.00	0.00	8.00
4-Year College	2.83	0.50	0.00	15.00
MA/PHD Granting Institution	6.70	0.00	0.00	56.00
Research University	7.00	3.00	0.00	20.00

Table 17.4 How many computers does the library have that can dual boot Apple and Microsoft operating systems? Broken out by Public Versus Private

Public Versus Private	Mean	Median	Minimum	Maximum
Public	4.88	0.00	0.00	56.00
Private	1.64	0.00	0.00	15.00

Table 17.5 How many computers does the library have that can dual boot Apple and Microsoft operating systems? Broken out by Total Annual Enrollment

Total Annual Enrollment	Mean	Median	Minimum	Maximum
2,000 or less	1.13	0.00	0.00	8.00
2,000 – 10,000	1.06	0.00	0.00	15.00
More than 10,000	9.91	3.00	0.00	56.00

Table 17.6 How many computers does the library have that can dual boot Apple and Microsoft operating systems? Broken out by Total Annual Tuition

Total Annual Tuition	Mean	Median	Minimum	Maximum
Less than $5,000	0.77	0.00	0.00	8.00
$5,000 - $20,000	4.40	0.50	0.00	20.00
More than $20,000	6.75	0.00	0.00	56.00

Table 18.1 How many dual-boot computers able to run both Apple and Windows software does it plan to purchase over the next year?

	Mean	Median	Minimum	Maximum
Entire sample	0.35	0.00	0.00	4.00

Table 18.2 How many dual-boot computers able to run both Apple and Windows software does it plan to purchase over the next year? Broken out by Level of authority when making decisions about the purchase of new computer technologies

Level of authority when making decisions about the purchase of new computer technologies	Mean	Median	Minimum	Maximum
Recommend only	0.00	0.00	0.00	0.00
Need approval	0.67	0.00	0.00	4.00
Have authority to buy	0.56	0.00	0.00	3.00

Table 18.3 How many dual-boot computers able to run both Apple and Windows software does it plan to purchase over the next year? Broken out by Carnegie Class

Carnegie Class	Mean	Median	Minimum	Maximum
Community College	0.29	0.00	0.00	4.00
4-Year College	0.40	0.00	0.00	2.00
MA/PHD Granting Institution	0.00	0.00	0.00	0.00
Research University	1.25	1.00	0.00	3.00

Table 18.4 How many dual-boot computers able to run both Apple and Windows software does it plan to purchase over the next year? Broken out by Public Versus Private

Public Versus Private	Mean	Median	Minimum	Maximum
Public	0.41	0.00	0.00	4.00
Private	0.22	0.00	0.00	2.00

Table 18.5 How many dual-boot computers able to run both Apple and Windows software does it plan to purchase over the next year? Broken out by Total Annual Enrollment

Total Annual Enrollment	Mean	Median	Minimum	Maximum
2,000 or less	0.75	0.00	0.00	4.00
2,000 – 10,000	0.00	0.00	0.00	0.00
More than 10,000	0.56	0.00	0.00	3.00

Table 18.6 How many dual-boot computers able to run both Apple and Windows software does it plan to purchase over the next year? Broken out by Total Annual Tuition

Total Annual Tuition	Mean	Median	Minimum	Maximum
Less than $5,000	0.15	0.00	0.00	2.00
$5,000 - $20,000	0.56	0.00	0.00	3.00
More than $20,000	0.44	0.00	0.00	4.00

Table 18.7 Describe your computer tablet purchasing plans. Do you plan to make any such purchases for your library? Which vendors are you considering and why? How do you think it will impact computer use at the library?

1. We're not planning to buy anything this coming year.
2. We're currently not planning on purchasing any tablets in the upcoming fiscal cycles.
3. Yes, purchasing primarily for staff productivity. Considering patron use if accidental damage agreements can be negotiated. Apple and Google - primarily for ease of use/updating.
4. No explicit plans. Have experimented with Samsung and iPad tablets (20 total) for faculty and staff. No plans at this time to expand.
5. We have no plans to purchase tablet computers at present.
6. No plans, all our students have iPads as well as all our staff.
7. No plans at this time.
8. No plans this year or next. Apple.
9. We have no plans to purchase more tablets. We own two iPads and 6 Kindle Fires, which are included as tablets (they sort of straddle the line of eBook and tablet).
10. We are considering purchasing Kindle HDs and Apple iPads.
11. Director wants all librarians to have an iPad. Mainly so that we are able to help patrons who have them. At our institution, very few of our students can afford them. Therefore, I'm skeptical. Also, our networking issues are notoriously difficult for anything but "normal" PC and only recently the newer Macs. I have a personal Zenbook by ASUS and spent an hour and a half trying to log onto our network in order to remote desktop with my office computer. Impossible. I worry that our institution isn't willing/able to make the kind of structural investments necessarily for the newer technologies that will eventually come our way.
12. No plans to purchase computer tablets.
13. We will purchase Apple iPads for faculty and staff who wish to use one. We will buy one Windows 8 tablet for an IT tech in the library. These are used to complement, not replace, laptops.
14. No practical use for them for staff work, no consensus on importance for student instruction, do not currently lend technology to patrons therefore do not plan to buy tablets this year.
15. None currently - we need to upgrade the regular computers first.
16. Do not plan to purchase tablets in the near future. No budget.
17. Yes. Will use state approved vendors. Yes, we have already seen an impact in students who use their own devices instead of library computers. This will continue to increase. But many students still use our computers.
18. We are working cooperatively with IT for a campus-wide plan.
19. Yes. What our IT department says we can order. I'm hoping to roll it out a little at a time, so probably not much impact.
20. Library staff has had tablets purchased for us recently. We plan to try to implement

a tablet lending program by the fall. We will start with 4-5 iPads and maybe one Android tablet. We do not expect it to impact computer use in any way.

21. Purchase for selected staff – Apple.
22. No plans to purchase.
23. We haven't purchased many tablet computers but plan to purchase 2 or 3 for staff use.
24. IPads for eBook purchases.
25. I would like it if we could buy tablets, but it is probably not going to happen. Some of our students have their own and can access our online resources through them.
26. We are in the early stages of evaluating one iPad, and may consider purchasing more at a later date. The desired impact would be to move patrons away from fixed desktop locations an allow them to roam the library.
27. We plan to purchase one tablet to use for outcomes assessment at the reference desk.
28. We are not planning on purchasing more tablets. We purchased one iPad and have had limited use. One of the goals of the purchase was to test out eBooks through our database vendors.

Chapter 2. eBook Reading Devices

Table 19.1 What is the library's total stock of dedicated eBook reading devices (exclude general computer workstations and laptops).

	Mean	Median	Minimum	Maximum
Entire sample	3.66	0.00	0.00	49.00

Table 19.2 What is the library's total stock of dedicated eBook reading devices (exclude general computer workstations and laptops). Broken out by Level of authority when making decisions about the purchase of new computer technologies

Level of authority when making decisions about the purchase of new computer technologies	Mean	Median	Minimum	Maximum
Recommend only	3.08	0.00	0.00	16.00
Need approval	0.73	0.00	0.00	3.00
Have authority to buy	7.27	0.00	0.00	49.00

Table 19.3 What is the library's total stock of dedicated eBook reading devices (exclude general computer workstations and laptops). Broken out by Carnegie Class

Carnegie Class	Mean	Median	Minimum	Maximum
Community Collcgc	2.21	0.00	0.00	16.00
4-Year College	8.50	0.00	0.00	49.00
MA/PHD Granting	1.80	0.50	0.00	6.00

Institution				
Research University	5.60	3.00	0.00	20.00

Table 19.4 What is the library's total stock of dedicated eBook reading devices (exclude general computer workstations and laptops). Broken out by Public Versus Private

Public Versus Private	Mean	Median	Minimum	Maximum
Public	2.75	0.00	0.00	20.00
Private	5.64	0.00	0.00	49.00

Table 19.5 What is the library's total stock of dedicated eBook reading devices (exclude general computer workstations and laptops). Broken out by Total Annual Enrollment

Total Annual Enrollment	Mean	Median	Minimum	Maximum
2,000 or less	7.00	0.00	0.00	49.00
2,000 – 10,000	0.69	0.00	0.00	6.00
More than 10,000	5.55	3.00	0.00	20.00

Table 1.6 What is the library's total stock of dedicated eBook reading devices (exclude general computer workstations and laptops). Broken out by Total Annual Tuition

Total Annual Tuition	Mean	Median	Minimum	Maximum
Less than $5,000	2.62	0.00	0.00	16.00
$5,000 - $20,000	8.20	1.00	0.00	49.00
More than $20,000	1.00	0.00	0.00	6.00

Table 20 How much did (will) the library spend on eBook reading devices in the years specified:

Table 20.1.1 Amount spent on eBook reading devices in 2012-13

	Mean	Median	Minimum	Maximum
Entire sample	$165.79	$0.00	$0.00	$1,851.00

Table 20.1.2 Amount spent on eBook reading devices in 2012-13 Broken out by Level of authority when making decisions about the purchase of new computer technologies

Level of authority when making decisions about the purchase of new computer technologies	Mean	Median	Minimum	Maximum
Recommend only	$319.31	$0.00	$0.00	$1,851.00
Need approval	$92.00	$0.00	$0.00	$800.00
Have authority to buy	$40.00	$0.00	$0.00	$400.00

Table 20.1.3 Amount spent on eBook reading devices in 2012-13 Broken out by Carnegie Class

Carnegie Class	Mean	Median	Minimum	Maximum
Community College	$189.36	$0.00	$0.00	$1,851.00
4-Year College	$0.00	$0.00	$0.00	$0.00
MA/PHD Granting Institution	$162.00	$0.00	$0.00	$1,200.00
Research University	$300.00	$200.00	$0.00	$800.00

Table 20.1.4 Amount spent on eBook reading devices in 2012-13 Broken out by Public Versus Private

Public Versus Private	Mean	Median	Minimum	Maximum
Public	$167.43	$0.00	$0.00	$1,851.00
Private	$162.00	$0.00	$0.00	$1,200.00

Table 20.1.5 Amount spent on eBook reading devices in 2012-13 Broken out by Total Annual Enrollment

Total Annual Enrollment	Mean	Median	Minimum	Maximum
2,000 or less	$137.50	$0.00	$0.00	$800.00
2,000 – 10,000	$88.00	$0.00	$0.00	$1,200.00
More than 10,000	$305.10	$0.00	$0.00	$1,851.00

Table 20.1.6 Amount spent on eBook reading devices in 2012-13 Broken out by Total Annual Tuition

Total Annual Tuition	Mean	Median	Minimum	Maximum
Less than $5,000	$265.46	$0.00	$0.00	$1,851.00
$5,000 - $20,000	$77.78	$0.00	$0.00	$400.00
More than $20,000	$120.00	$0.00	$0.00	$1,200.00

Table 20.2.1 Amount spent on eBook reading devices in 2013-14 (anticipated)

	Mean	Median	Minimum	Maximum
Entire sample	$226.47	$0.00	$0.00	$5,000.00

Table 20.2.2 Amount spent on eBook reading devices in 2013-14 (anticipated) Broken out by Level of authority when making decisions about the purchase of new computer technologies

Level of authority when making decisions about the purchase of new computer technologies	Mean	Median	Minimum	Maximum
Recommend only	$38.46	$0.00	$0.00	$500.00
Need approval	$163.64	$0.00	$0.00	$1,000.00
Have authority to buy	$540.00	$0.00	$0.00	$5,000.00

Table 20.2.3 Amount spent on eBook reading devices in 2013-14 (anticipated) Broken out by Carnegie Class

Carnegie Class	Mean	Median	Minimum	Maximum
Community College	$107.14	$0.00	$0.00	$1,000.00
4-Year College	$833.33	$0.00	$0.00	$5,000.00
MA/PHD Granting Institution	$0.00	$0.00	$0.00	$0.00
Research University	$300.00	$200.00	$0.00	$800.00

Table 20.2.4 Amount spent on eBook reading devices in 2013-14 (anticipated) Broken out by Public Versus Private

Public Versus Private	Mean	Median	Minimum	Maximum
Public	$117.39	$0.00	$0.00	$1,000.00
Private	$454.55	$0.00	$0.00	$5,000.00

Table 20.2.5 Amount spent on eBook reading devices in 2013-14 (anticipated) Broken out by Total Annual Enrollment

Total Annual Enrollment	Mean	Median	Minimum	Maximum
2,000 or less	$812.50	$0.00	$0.00	$5,000.00
2,000 – 10,000	$0.00	$0.00	$0.00	$0.00
More than 10,000	$120.00	$0.00	$0.00	$800.00

Table 20.2.6 Amount spent on eBook reading devices in 2013-14 (anticipated) Broken out by Total Annual Tuition

Total Annual Tuition	Mean	Median	Minimum	Maximum
Less than $5,000	$176.92	$0.00	$0.00	$1,000.00
$5,000 - $20,000	$600.00	$0.00	$0.00	$5,000.00
More than $20,000	$0.00	$0.00	$0.00	$0.00

Table 21 Does the library currently own or lease any of the following

Table 21.1.1 Does the library currently own or lease an Amazon Kindle?

	Yes	No
Entire sample	31.43%	68.57%

Table 21.1.2 Does the library currently own or lease an Amazon Kindle? Broken out by Level of authority when making decisions about the purchase of new computer technologies

Level of authority when making decisions about the purchase of new computer technologies	Yes	No
Recommend only	38.46%	61.54%
Need approval	27.27%	72.73%
Have authority to buy	27.27%	72.73%

Table 21.1.3 Does the library currently own or lease an Amazon Kindle? Broken out by Carnegie Class

Carnegie Class	No Answer	Yes
Community College	78.57%	21.43%
4-Year College	83.33%	16.67%
MA/PHD Granting Institution	60.00%	40.00%
Research University	40.00%	60.00%

Table 21.1.4 Does the library currently own or lease an Amazon Kindle? Broken out by Public Versus Private

Public Versus Private	No Answer	Yes
Public	66.67%	33.33%
Private	72.73%	27.27%

Table 21.1.5 Does the library currently own or lease an Amazon Kindle? Broken out by Total Annual Enrollment

Total Annual Enrollment	Yes	No
2,000 or less	12.50%	87.50%
2,000 – 10,000	18.75%	81.25%
More than 10,000	63.64%	36.36%

Table 21.1.6 Does the library currently own or lease an Amazon Kindle? Broken out by Total Annual Tuition

Total Annual Tuition	Yes	No
Less than $5,000	30.77%	69.23%
$5,000 - $20,000	30.00%	70.00%
More than $20,000	33.33%	66.67%

Table 21.3.1 Does the library currently own or lease a Barnes and Noble Nook?

	Yes	No
Entire sample	17.14%	82.86%

Table 21.3.2 Does the library currently own or lease a Barnes and Noble Nook? Broken out by Level of authority when making decisions about the purchase of new computer technologies

Level of authority when making decisions about the purchase of new computer technologies	Yes	No
Recommend only	23.08%	76.92%
Need approval	9.09%	90.91%
Have authority to buy	18.18%	81.82%

Table 21.3.3 Does the library currently own or lease a Barnes and Noble Nook? Broken out by Carnegie Class

Carnegie Class	Yes	No
Community College	14.29%	85.71%
4-Year College	0.00%	100.00%
MA/PHD Granting Institution	20.00%	80.00%
Research University	40.00%	60.00%

Table 21.3.4 Does the library currently own or lease a Barnes and Noble Nook Broken out by Public Versus Private

Public Versus Private	Yes	No
Public	20.83%	79.17%
Private	9.09%	90.91%

Table 21.3.5 Does the library currently own or lease a Barnes and Noble Nook Broken out by Total Annual Enrollment

Total Annual Enrollment	Yes	No
2,000 or less	25.00%	75.00%
2,000 – 10,000	0.00%	100.00%
More than 10,000	36.36%	63.64%

Table 21.3.6 Does the library currently own or lease a Barnes and Noble Nook Broken out by Total Annual Tuition

Total Annual Tuition	Yes	No
Less than $5,000	23.08%	76.92%
$5,000 - $20,000	30.00%	70.00%
More than $20,000	0.00%	100.00%

Table 22 Does the library plan to purchase any of the following over the next two years?

Table 22.1.1 Plans to purchase an Amazon Kindle over the next two years

	Yes	No
Entire sample	5.71%	94.29%

Table 22.1.2 Plans to purchase an Amazon Kindle over the next two years Broken out by Level of authority when making decisions about the purchase of new computer technologies

Level of authority when making decisions about the purchase of new computer technologies	Yes	No
Recommend only	7.69%	92.31%
Need approval	9.09%	90.91%
Have authority to buy	0.00%	100.00%

Table 22.1.3 Plans to purchase an Amazon Kindle over the next two years Broken out by Carnegie Class

Carnegie Class	Yes	No
Community College	7.14%	92.86%
4-Year College	0.00%	100.00%
MA/PHD Granting Institution	0.00%	100.00%
Research University	20.00%	80.00%

Table 22.1.4 Plans to purchase an Amazon Kindle over the next two years Broken out by Public Versus Private

Public Versus Private	Yes	No
Public	8.33%	91.67%
Private	0.00%	100.00%

Table 22.1.5 Amazon Kindle Broken out by Total Annual Enrollment

Total Annual Enrollment	Yes	No
2,000 or less	12.50%	87.50%
2,000 – 10,000	0.00%	100.00%
More than 10,000	9.09%	90.91%

Table 22.1. Plans to purchase an Amazon Kindle over the next two years Broken out by Total Annual Tuition

Total Annual Tuition	Yes	No
Less than $5,000	15.38%	84.62%
$5,000 - $20,000	0.00%	100.00%
More than $20,000	0.00%	100.00%

Table 22.2.1 Plans to purchase a Sony Reader over the next two years

	Yes	No
Entire sample	2.86%	97.14%

Table 22.2.2 Plans to purchase a Sony Reader over the next two years Broken out by Level of authority when making decisions about the purchase of new computer technologies

Level of authority when making decisions about the purchase of new computer technologies	Yes	No
Recommend only	0.00%	100.00%
Need approval	9.09%	90.91%
Have authority to buy	0.00%	100.00%

Table 22.2.3 Plans to purchase a Sony Reader over the next two years Broken out by Carnegie Class

Carnegie Class	Yes	No
Community College	0.00%	100.00%
4-Year College	0.00%	100.00%
MA/PHD Granting Institution	0.00%	100.00%
Research University	20.00%	80.00%

Table 22.2.4 Plans to purchase a Sony Reader over the next two years Broken out by Public Versus Private

Public Versus Private	Yes	No
Public	4.17%	95.83%
Private	0.00%	100.00%

Table 22.2.5 Plans to purchase a Sony Reader over the next two years Broken out by Total Annual Enrollment

Total Annual Enrollment	Yes	No
2,000 or less	0.00%	100.00%
2,000 – 10,000	0.00%	100.00%
More than 10,000	9.09%	90.91%

Table 22.2.6 Plans to purchase a Sony Reader over the next two years Broken out by Total Annual Tuition

Total Annual Tuition	Yes	No
Less than $5,000	7.69%	92.31%
$5,000 - $20,000	0.00%	100.00%
More than $20,000	0.00%	100.00%

Table 22.3.1 Plans to purchase a Barnes and Noble Nook over the next two years

	Yes	No
Entire sample	2.86%	97.14%

Table 22.3.2 Plans to purchase a Barnes and Noble Nook over the next two years Broken out by Level of authority when making decisions about the purchase of new computer technologies

Level of authority when making decisions about the purchase of new computer technologies	Yes	No
Recommend only	0.00%	100.00%
Need approval	9.09%	90.91%
Have authority to buy	0.00%	100.00%

Table 22.3.3 Plans to purchase a Barnes and Noble Nook over the next two years Broken out by Carnegie Class

Carnegie Class	Yes	No
Community College	0.00%	100.00%
4-Year College	0.00%	100.00%
MA/PHD Granting Institution	0.00%	100.00%
Research University	20.00%	80.00%

Table 22.3.4 Plans to purchase a Barnes and Noble Nook over the next two years Broken out by Public Versus Private

Public Versus Private	Yes	No
Public	4.17%	95.83%
Private	0.00%	100.00%

Table 22.3.5 Plans to purchase a Barnes and Noble Nook over the next two years Broken out by Total Annual Enrollment

Total Annual Enrollment	Yes	No
2,000 or less	0.00%	100.00%
2,000 – 10,000	0.00%	100.00%
More than 10,000	9.09%	90.91%

Table 22.3.6 Plans to purchase a Barnes and Noble Nook over the next two years Broken out by Total Annual Tuition

Total Annual Tuition	Yes	No
Less than $5,000	7.69%	92.31%
$5,000 - $20,000	0.00%	100.00%
More than $20,000	0.00%	100.00%

Chapter 3. Information Technology Staffing

Table 23 How many of the following does the library (or Information Technology Department if it controls this function) employ on the library technology help desk:

Table 23.1.1 Number of Full time Staffers employed on the library technology help desk

	Mean	Median	Minimum	Maximum
Entire sample	2.04	1.00	0.00	13.00

Table 23.1.2 Number of Full time Staffers employed on the library technology help desk Broken out by Level of authority when making decisions about the purchase of new computer technologies

Level of authority when making decisions about the purchase of new computer technologies	Mean	Median	Minimum	Maximum
Recommend only	2.22	1.00	0.00	13.00
Need approval	1.00	1.00	0.00	2.00
Have authority to buy	2.78	2.00	0.00	6.00

Table 23.1.3 Number of Full time Staffers employed on the library technology help desk Broken out by Carnegie Class

Carnegie Class	Mean	Median	Minimum	Maximum
Community College	2.00	1.00	0.00	13.00
4-Year College	1.00	1.00	0.00	2.00
MA/PHD Granting Institution	1.80	0.00	0.00	6.00
Research University	3.40	3.00	1.00	6.00

Table 23.1.4 Number of Full time Staffers employed on the library technology help desk Broken out by Public Versus Private

Public Versus Private	Mean	Median	Minimum	Maximum
Public	2.40	1.00	0.00	13.00
Private	0.83	1.00	0.00	2.00

Table 23.1.5 Number of Full time Staffers employed on the library technology help desk Broken out by Total Annual Enrollment

Total Annual Enrollment	Mean	Median	Minimum	Maximum
2,000 or less	0.71	1.00	0.00	2.00
2,000 – 10,000	0.78	1.00	0.00	2.00
More than 10,000	4.10	3.00	0.00	13.00

Table 23.1.6 Number of Full time Staffers employed on the library technology help desk Broken out by Total Annual Tuition

Total Annual Tuition	Mean	Median	Minimum	Maximum
Less than $5,000	2.10	1.00	0.00	13.00
$5,000 - $20,000	3.00	2.00	0.00	6.00
More than $20,000	1.00	1.00	0.00	3.00

Table 23.2.1 Number of Part Time Staffers employed on the library technology help desk

	Mean	Median	Minimum	Maximum
Entire sample	6.83	0.00	0.00	70.00

Table 23.2.2 Number of Part Time Staffers employed on the library technology help desk Broken out by Level of authority when making decisions about the purchase of new computer technologies

Level of authority when making decisions about the purchase of new computer technologies	Mean	Median	Minimum	Maximum
Recommend only	1.44	0.00	0.00	6.00
Need approval	1.48	0.00	0.00	8.00
Have authority to buy	19.86	0.00	0.00	70.00

Table 23.2.3 Number of Part Time Staffers employed on the library technology help desk Broken out by Carnegie Class

Carnegie Class	Mean	Median	Minimum	Maximum
Community College	1.18	0.00	0.00	6.00
4-Year College	0.83	0.00	0.00	5.00
MA/PHD Granting Institution	23.83	4.00	0.00	70.00
Research University	2.00	2.00	0.00	4.00

Table 23.2.4 Number of Part Time Staffers employed on the library technology help desk Broken out by Public Versus Private

Public Versus Private	Mean	Median	Minimum	Maximum
Public	9.43	0.00	0.00	70.00
Private	1.63	0.00	0.00	8.00

Table 23.2.5 Number of Part Time Staffers employed on the library technology help desk Broken out by Total Annual Enrollment

Total Annual Enrollment	Mean	Median	Minimum	Maximum
2,000 or less	0.54	0.00	0.00	3.00
2,000 – 10,000	1.36	0.00	0.00	8.00
More than 10,000	24.17	5.00	0.00	70.00

Table 23.2.6 Number of Part Time Staffers employed on the library technology help desk Broken out by Total Annual Tuition

Total Annual Tuition	Mean	Median	Minimum	Maximum
Less than $5,000	0.85	0.00	0.00	6.00
$5,000 - $20,000	11.83	1.00	0.00	65.00
More than $20,000	8.60	0.00	0.00	70.00

Table 24.1 What is total estimated spending for the total annual salaries of full and part time staffers for the library technology help desk?

	Mean	Median	Minimum	Maximum
Entire sample	$99,352.75	$31,000.00	$0.00	$550,000.00

Table 24.2 What is total estimated spending for the total annual salaries of full and part time staffers for the library technology help desk? Broken out by Level of authority when making decisions about the purchase of new computer technologies

Level of authority when making decisions about the purchase of new computer technologies	Mean	Median	Minimum	Maximum
Recommend only	$46,428.57	$0.00	$0.00	$240,000.00
Need approval	$34,011.00	$55.00	$0.00	$90,000.00
Have authority to buy	$186,500.00	$90,000.00	$0.00	$550,000.00

Table 24.3 What is total estimated spending for the total annual salaries of full and part time staffers for the library technology help desk? Broken out by Carnegie Class

Carnegie Class	Mean	Median	Minimum	Maximum
Community College	$28,857.14	$0.00	$0.00	$90,000.00
4-Year College	$28,763.75	$15,027.50	$0.00	$85,000.00
MA/PHD Granting Institution	$148,000.00	$0.00	$0.00	$500,000.00
Research University	$232,500.00	$160,000.00	$60,000.00	$550,000.00

Table 24.4 What is total estimated spending for the total annual salaries of full and part time staffers for the library technology help desk? Broken out by Public Versus Private

Public Versus Private	Mean	Median	Minimum	Maximum
Public	$133,714.29	$70,000.00	$0.00	$550,000.00
Private	$19,175.83	$27.50	$0.00	$85,000.00

Table 24.5 What is total estimated spending for the total annual salaries of full and part time staffers for the library technology help desk? Broken out by Total Annual Enrollment

Total Annual Enrollment	Mean	Median	Minimum	Maximum
2,000 or less	$29,000.00	$15,000.00	$0.00	$90,000.00
2,000 – 10,000	$14,175.83	$0.00	$0.00	$85,000.00
More than 10,000	$278,333.33	$220,000.00	$60,000.00	$550,000.00

Table 24.6 What is total estimated spending for the total annual salaries of full and part time staffers for the library technology help desk? Broken out by Total Annual Tuition

Total Annual Tuition	Mean	Median	Minimum	Maximum
Less than $5,000	$20,333.33	$0.00	$0.00	$90,000.00
$5,000 - $20,000	$137,142.86	$60,000.00	$0.00	$550,000.00
More than $20,000	$129,293.57	$80,000.00	$0.00	$500,000.00

Table 24.7 Compare the ease of maintenance of desktop computers with laptop and tablet computers? Which are the most difficult to maintain? Over which do you incur the most maintenance costs in dollars and staff time? Are there hidden costs or savings in deploying one type of computer over another? Or one brand over another? Explain.

1. Have had nothing but trouble with the desktops. Don't know about the laptops.
2. Laptops are higher maintenance and cost more. Power cords break, wireless can be unreliable.
3. Laptops cost more to buy and require more support simply because they are mobile. Laptops users also attempt to do things that fixed workstation users don't. In our environment, Mac laptops and ultrabooks have greater support costs because they don't integrate well with our support infrastructure.
4. Desktop less overhead, easier to manage remotely. In process of moving out of the laptop loan service, largely due to limited unique users and high maintenance costs-- re-image after each loan.
5. Because the laptops are cleaned and inspected whenever they're returned, they take more staff time than desktop machines.
6. Desktops are more easily repaired, more accessible and more easily upgraded.
7. We have two people who work at the library. We both serve all library patrons regardless if it is a "library" question or technology question. We have an IT service technician for anything we can't do. Mac devices take the most time because we are not familiar with them.
8. Desktops are a piece of cake compared to laptops.
9. We offer only desk tops. We used to rent laptops, but the cost in staff time was prohibitive.
10. Laptops most difficult to maintain. Apple is so dependable we hardly ever have a repair problem.
11. Maintenance of desktop computers is easier. We have not really purchased laptops for the library, as students can loan them from Books in Print.
12. It is easier to deal with the tablets, but both laptops and desktops are not significantly more difficult. Probably most maintenance cost for desktops. Tablets require a lot of tech help over the phone and by email. Kindles are notoriously difficult with accessing academic library material.
13. Again, our IT department maintains things when there are problems. But, we tend not to have hardware problems. We have wireless connectivity issues (our building is 60+ years old), electrical outlet/power problems, network stuff. We librarians do not have the expertise, nor the authority to handle most of the computing issues we experience in the building. Truthfully, the Dell machines rarely give us problems... our Macs (all 8 of them) seem somewhat more temperamental. But, we don't have good tech support for them either.
14. The university's Division of Technology Services maintains our computers; this is not a library function.

15. Desktops are easier to upgrade and repair - we can add hard drives, memory, video cards, etc. Laptops are more difficult but we can do them. We can connect remotely to both laptops and desktop machine to update software, remove viruses, etc. Tablets take relatively more time because they have to be updated one-by-one.
16. Desktops much easier because we have a large number so can swap parts in and out to keep unit working; if one thing breaks in a laptop it is unusable for a longer period of time. Biggest problem/issue with laptops is recharge time required for battery - laptop cannot be used for continuous all day untethered activities.
17. Laptops and tablets are the most difficult to maintain. More difficult to push out/automate installs, updates on laptops and tablets, especially if not connected to the network.
18. Laptops, but just because they are loaned out to students and must be wiped clean individually. Our other student computers are collectively wiped clean (Deep Freeze) every evening.
19. Clone out bad hard drives is most difficult. One type of PC makes maintenance easier.
20. The laptops have been the more problematic and have to be taken to IT quite often. The desktops are only problematic if IT hasn't pushed the updates out like they need to for some software. The desktops are the most reliable and will be for quite some time.
21. Laptops incur more maintenance costs mainly due to batteries needing to be replaced before the laptop reaches the replacement cycle.
22. Our IT dept. handles maintenance. Most of our computers are desktops; the few laptops we have are treated the same as the public desktops. Haven't noticed any differences or issues of one over the other.
23. Maintenance is handled by a different division of the college.
24. The problem with maintaining laptops is that they are used outside the university network. It is critical that that the virus software be kept up to date.
25. No difference in maintenance.
26. Desktop computers are easier to maintain because the parts are interchangeable. However, I think it's also important to adapt to the times. The business world is shifting away from desktop computers. Laptops and tablets also allow mobility throughout the library, which allows us to maximize the utilization of our resources.

Chapter 4. Technology Training

Table 25 Rate the following tools for the extent to which they help the library to educate patrons about computer technology in the library.

Table 25.1.1 Usefulness of videos made by the library about library computer technology in educating patrons about computer technology in the library

	No Answer	Not useful	Somewhat useful	Useful	Very useful	Do not use
Entire sample	5.71%	31.43%	5.71%	22.86%	28.57%	5.71%

Table 25.1.2 Usefulness of videos made by the library about library computer technology in educating patrons about computer technology in the library Broken out by Level of authority when making decisions about the purchase of new computer technologies

Level of authority when making decisions about the purchase of new computer technologies	No Answer	Not useful	Somewhat useful	Useful	Very useful	Do not use
Recommend only	0.00%	38.46%	7.69%	15.38%	30.77%	7.69%
Need approval	9.09%	18.18%	0.00%	36.36%	36.36%	0.00%
Have authority to buy	9.09%	36.36%	9.09%	18.18%	18.18%	9.09%

Table 25.1.3 Usefulness of videos made by the library about library computer technology in educating patrons about computer technology in the library Broken out by Carnegie Class

Carnegie Class	No Answer	Not useful	Somewhat useful	Useful	Very useful	Do not use
Community College	0.00%	14.29%	7.14%	28.57%	42.86%	7.14%
4-Year College	0.00%	50.00%	0.00%	50.00%	0.00%	0.00%
MA/PHD Granting Institution	10.00%	40.00%	10.00%	0.00%	30.00%	10.00%
Research University	20.00%	40.00%	0.00%	20.00%	20.00%	0.00%

Table 25.1.4 Usefulness of videos made by the library about library computer technology in educating patrons about computer technology in the library Broken out by Public Versus Private

Public Versus Private	No Answer	Not useful	Somewhat useful	Useful	Very useful	Do not use
Public	4.17%	29.17%	8.33%	20.83%	29.17%	8.33%
Private	9.09%	36.36%	0.00%	27.27%	27.27%	0.00%

Table 25.1.5 Usefulness of videos made by the library about library computer technology in educating patrons about computer technology in the library Broken out by Total Annual Enrollment

Total Annual Enrollment	No Answer	Not useful	Somewhat useful	Useful	Very useful	Do not use
2,000 or less	0.00%	25.00%	0.00%	37.50%	25.00%	12.50%
2,000 – 10,000	6.25%	31.25%	6.25%	25.00%	31.25%	0.00%
More than 10,000	9.09%	36.36%	9.09%	9.09%	27.27%	9.09%

Table 25.1.6 Usefulness of videos made by the library about library computer technology in educating patrons about computer technology in the library Broken out by Total Annual Tuition

Total Annual Tuition	No Answer	Not useful	Somewhat useful	Useful	Very useful	Do not use
Less than $5,000	0.00%	15.38%	7.69%	30.77%	38.46%	7.69%
$5,000 - $20,000	10.00%	50.00%	10.00%	20.00%	10.00%	0.00%
More than $20,000	8.33%	33.33%	0.00%	16.67%	33.33%	8.33%

Table 25.2.1 Usefulness of videos made by manufacturers about their products in educating patrons about computer technology in the library

	No Answer	Not useful	Somewhat useful	Useful	Very useful	Do not use
Entire sample	5.71%	37.14%	5.71%	22.86%	20.00%	8.57%

Table 25.2.2 Usefulness of videos made by manufacturers about their products in educating patrons about computer technology in the library Broken out by Level of authority when making decisions about the purchase of new computer technologies

Level of authority when making decisions about the purchase of new computer technologies	No Answer	Not useful	Somewhat useful	Useful	Very useful	Do not use
Recommend only	0.00%	46.15%	7.69%	15.38%	15.38%	15.38%
Need approval	9.09%	18.18%	0.00%	45.45%	18.18%	9.09%
Have authority to buy	9.09%	45.45%	9.09%	9.09%	27.27%	0.00%

Table 25.2.3 Usefulness of videos made by manufacturers about their products in educating patrons about computer technology in the library Broken out by Carnegie Class

Carnegie Class	No Answer	Not useful	Somewhat useful	Useful	Very useful	Do not use
Community College	0.00%	14.29%	7.14%	42.86%	21.43%	14.29%
4-Year College	0.00%	50.00%	0.00%	33.33%	16.67%	0.00%
MA/PHD Granting Institution	10.00%	60.00%	10.00%	0.00%	10.00%	10.00%
Research University	20.00%	40.00%	0.00%	0.00%	40.00%	0.00%

Table 25.2.4 Usefulness of videos made by manufacturers about their products in educating patrons about computer technology in the library Broken out by Public Versus Private

Public Versus Private	No Answer	Not useful	Somewhat useful	Useful	Very useful	Do not use
Public	4.17%	33.33%	8.33%	25.00%	20.83%	8.33%
Private	9.09%	45.45%	0.00%	18.18%	18.18%	9.09%

Table 25.2.5 Usefulness of videos made by manufacturers about their products in educating patrons about computer technology in the library Broken out by Total Annual Enrollment

Total Annual Enrollment	No Answer	Not useful	Somewhat useful	Useful	Very useful	Do not use
2,000 or less	0.00%	12.50%	0.00%	50.00%	25.00%	12.50%
2,000 – 10,000	6.25%	43.75%	6.25%	18.75%	12.50%	12.50%
More than 10,000	9.09%	45.45%	9.09%	9.09%	27.27%	0.00%

Table 25.2.6 Usefulness of videos made by manufacturers about their products in educating patrons about computer technology in the library Broken out by Total Annual Tuition

Total Annual Tuition	No Answer	Not useful	Somewhat useful	Useful	Very useful	Do not use
Less than $5,000	0.00%	7.69%	7.69%	46.15%	23.08%	15.38%
$5,000 - $20,000	10.00%	60.00%	10.00%	0.00%	20.00%	0.00%
More than $20,000	8.33%	50.00%	0.00%	16.67%	16.67%	8.33%

Table 25.3.1 Usefulness of online tutorials made by the library in educating patrons about computer technology in the library

	No Answer	Not useful	Useful	Very useful	Do not use
Entire sample	5.71%	25.71%	20.00%	22.86%	25.71%

Table 25.3.2 Usefulness of online tutorials made by the library in educating patrons about computer technology in the library Broken out by Level of authority when making decisions about the purchase of new computer technologies

Level of authority when making decisions about the purchase of new computer technologies	No Answer	Not useful	Useful	Very useful	Do not use
Recommend only	0.00%	30.77%	7.69%	30.77%	30.77%
Need approval	9.09%	9.09%	36.36%	18.18%	27.27%
Have authority to buy	9.09%	36.36%	18.18%	18.18%	18.18%

Table 25.3.3 Usefulness of online tutorials made by the library in educating patrons about computer technology in the library Broken out by Carnegie Class

Carnegie Class	No Answer	Not useful	Useful	Very useful	Do not use
Community College	0.00%	14.29%	21.43%	28.57%	35.71%
4-Year College	0.00%	33.33%	50.00%	0.00%	16.67%
MA/PHD Granting Institution	10.00%	40.00%	10.00%	20.00%	20.00%
Research University	20.00%	20.00%	0.00%	40.00%	20.00%

Table 25.3.4 Usefulness of online tutorials made by the library in educating patrons about computer technology in the library Broken out by Public Versus Private

Public Versus Private	No Answer	Not useful	Useful	Very useful	Do not use
Public	4.17%	25.00%	16.67%	25.00%	29.17%
Private	9.09%	27.27%	27.27%	18.18%	18.18%

Table 25.3.5 Usefulness of online tutorials made by the library in educating patrons about computer technology in the library Broken out by Total Annual Enrollment

Total Annual Enrollment	No Answer	Not useful	Useful	Very useful	Do not use
2,000 or less	0.00%	37.50%	37.50%	25.00%	0.00%
2,000 - 10,000	6.25%	18.75%	25.00%	18.75%	31.25%
More than 10,000	9.09%	27.27%	0.00%	27.27%	36.36%

Table 25.3.6 Usefulness of online tutorials made by the library in educating patrons about computer technology in the library Broken out by Total Annual Tuition

Total Annual Tuition	No Answer	Not useful	Useful	Very useful	Do not use
Less than $5,000	0.00%	15.38%	23.08%	30.77%	30.77%
$5,000 - $20,000	10.00%	50.00%	10.00%	10.00%	20.00%
More than $20,000	8.33%	16.67%	25.00%	25.00%	25.00%

Table 25.4.1 Usefulness of Distribution of training or technology information through social networking sites such as Facebook or Twitter in educating patrons about computer technology in the library

	No Answer	Not useful	Somewhat useful	Useful	Very useful	Do not use
Entire sample	5.71%	37.14%	2.86%	31.43%	20.00%	2.86%

Table 25.4.2 Usefulness of Distribution of training or technology information through social networking sites such as Facebook or Twitter in educating patrons about computer technology in the library Broken out by Level of authority when making decisions about the purchase of new computer technologies

Level of authority when making decisions about the purchase of new computer technologies	No Answer	Not useful	Somewhat useful	Useful	Very useful	Do not use
Recommend only	0.00%	46.15%	7.69%	30.77%	7.69%	7.69%
Need approval	9.09%	27.27%	0.00%	36.36%	27.27%	0.00%
Have authority to buy	9.09%	36.36%	0.00%	27.27%	27.27%	0.00%

Table 25.4.3 Usefulness of Distribution of training or technology information through social networking sites such as Facebook or Twitter in educating patrons about computer technology in the library Broken out by Carnegie Class

Carnegie Class	No Answer	Not useful	Somewhat useful	Useful	Very useful	Do not use
Community College	0.00%	35.71%	0.00%	28.57%	28.57%	7.14%
4-Year College	0.00%	33.33%	16.67%	16.67%	33.33%	0.00%
MA/PHD Granting Institution	10.00%	40.00%	0.00%	40.00%	10.00%	0.00%
Research University	20.00%	40.00%	0.00%	40.00%	0.00%	0.00%

Table 25.4.4 Usefulness of Distribution of training or technology information through social networking sites such as Facebook or Twitter in educating patrons about computer technology in the library Broken out by Public Versus Private

Public Versus Private	No Answer	Not useful	Somewhat useful	Useful	Very useful	Do not use
Public	4.17%	41.67%	0.00%	33.33%	16.67%	4.17%
Private	9.09%	27.27%	9.09%	27.27%	27.27%	0.00%

Table 25.4.5 Usefulness of Distribution of training or technology information through social networking sites such as Facebook or Twitter in educating patrons about computer technology in the library Broken out by Total Annual Enrollment

Total Annual Enrollment	No Answer	Not useful	Somewhat useful	Useful	Very useful	Do not use
2,000 or less	0.00%	37.50%	0.00%	37.50%	25.00%	0.00%
2,000 – 10,000	6.25%	31.25%	6.25%	31.25%	25.00%	0.00%
More than 10,000	9.09%	45.45%	0.00%	27.27%	9.09%	9.09%

Table 25.4.6 Usefulness of Distribution of training or technology information through social networking sites such as Facebook or Twitter in educating patrons about computer technology in the library Broken out by Total Annual Tuition

Total Annual Tuition	No Answer	Not useful	Somewhat useful	Useful	Very useful	Do not use
Less than $5,000	0.00%	38.46%	0.00%	23.08%	30.77%	7.69%
$5,000 - $20,000	10.00%	50.00%	0.00%	30.00%	10.00%	0.00%
More than $20,000	8.33%	25.00%	8.33%	41.67%	16.67%	0.00%

Table 25.5.1 Usefulness of a library technology blog in educating patrons about computer technology in the library

	No Answer	Not useful	Somewhat useful	Useful	Very useful
Entire sample	5.71%	54.29%	14.29%	11.43%	14.29%

Table 25.5.2 Usefulness of a library technology blog in educating patrons about computer technology in the library Broken out by Level of authority when making decisions about the purchase of new computer technologies

Level of authority when making decisions about the purchase of new computer technologies	No Answer	Not useful	Somewhat useful	Useful	Very useful
Recommend only	0.00%	53.85%	15.38%	15.38%	15.38%
Need approval	9.09%	54.55%	18.18%	0.00%	18.18%
Have authority to buy	9.09%	54.55%	9.09%	18.18%	9.09%

Table 25.5.3 Usefulness of a library technology blog in educating patrons about computer technology in the library Broken out by Carnegie Class

Carnegie Class	No Answer	Not useful	Somewhat useful	Useful	Very useful
Community College	0.00%	35.71%	21.43%	14.29%	28.57%
4-Year College	0.00%	66.67%	16.67%	0.00%	16.67%
MA/PHD Granting Institution	10.00%	60.00%	10.00%	20.00%	0.00%
Research University	20.00%	80.00%	0.00%	0.00%	0.00%

Table 25.5.4 Usefulness of a library technology blog in educating patrons about computer technology in the library Broken out by Public Versus Private

Public Versus Private	No Answer	Not useful	Somewhat useful	Useful	Very useful
Public	4.17%	50.00%	16.67%	12.50%	16.67%
Private	9.09%	63.64%	9.09%	9.09%	9.09%

Table 25.5.5 Usefulness of a library technology blog in educating patrons about computer technology in the library Broken out by Total Annual Enrollment

Total Annual Enrollment	No Answer	Not useful	Somewhat useful	Useful	Very useful
2,000 or less	0.00%	50.00%	12.50%	12.50%	25.00%
2,000 – 10,000	6.25%	50.00%	18.75%	12.50%	12.50%
More than 10,000	9.09%	63.64%	9.09%	9.09%	9.09%

Table 25.5.6 Usefulness of a library technology blog in educating patrons about computer technology in the library Broken out by Total Annual Tuition

Total Annual Tuition	No Answer	Not useful	Somewhat useful	Useful	Very useful
Less than $5,000	0.00%	46.15%	23.08%	7.69%	23.08%
$5,000 - $20,000	10.00%	60.00%	10.00%	20.00%	0.00%
More than $20,000	8.33%	58.33%	8.33%	8.33%	16.67%

Table 25.6.1 Usefulness of Formal classes for students on library technology in educating patrons about computer technology in the library

	No Answer	Not useful	Useful	Very useful	Do not use
Entire sample	5.71%	28.57%	22.86%	22.86%	20.00%

Table 25.6.2 Usefulness of Formal classes for students on library technology in educating patrons about computer technology in the library Broken out by Level of authority when making decisions about the purchase of new computer technologies

Level of authority when making decisions about the purchase of new computer technologies	No Answer	Not useful	Useful	Very useful	Do not use
Recommend only	0.00%	38.46%	23.08%	23.08%	15.38%
Need approval	9.09%	27.27%	27.27%	18.18%	18.18%
Have authority to buy	9.09%	18.18%	18.18%	27.27%	27.27%

Table 25.6.3 Usefulness of Formal classes for students on library technology in educating patrons about computer technology in the library Broken out by Carnegie Class

Carnegie Class	No Answer	Not useful	Useful	Very useful	Do not use
Community College	0.00%	21.43%	21.43%	21.43%	35.71%
4-Year College	0.00%	33.33%	50.00%	0.00%	16.67%
MA/PHD Granting Institution	10.00%	40.00%	10.00%	30.00%	10.00%
Research University	20.00%	20.00%	20.00%	40.00%	0.00%

Table 25.6.4 Usefulness of Formal classes for students on library technology in educating patrons about computer technology in the library Broken out by Public Versus Private

Public Versus Private	No Answer	Not useful	Useful	Very useful	Do not use
Public	4.17%	25.00%	20.83%	25.00%	25.00%
Private	9.09%	36.36%	27.27%	18.18%	9.09%

Table 25.6.5 Usefulness of Formal classes for students on library technology in educating patrons about computer technology in the library Broken out by Total Annual Enrollment

Total Annual Enrollment	No Answer	Not useful	Useful	Very useful	Do not use
2,000 or less	0.00%	25.00%	25.00%	12.50%	37.50%
2,000 - 10,000	6.25%	37.50%	31.25%	18.75%	6.25%
More than 10,000	9.09%	18.18%	9.09%	36.36%	27.27%

Table 25.6.6 Usefulness of Formal classes for students on library technology in educating patrons about computer technology in the library Broken out by Total Annual Tuition

Total Annual Tuition	No Answer	Not useful	Useful	Very useful	Do not use
Less than $5,000	0.00%	15.38%	23.08%	23.08%	38.46%
$5,000 - $20,000	10.00%	40.00%	20.00%	20.00%	10.00%
More than $20,000	8.33%	33.33%	25.00%	25.00%	8.33%

Table 25.7.1 Usefulness of Print Handouts Describing Library Technology in educating patrons about computer technology in the library

	No Answer	Not useful	Useful	Very useful	Do not use
Entire sample	5.71%	22.86%	40.00%	22.86%	8.57%

Table 25.7.2 Usefulness of Print Handouts Describing Library Technology in educating patrons about computer technology in the library Broken out by Level of authority when making decisions about the purchase of new computer technologies

Level of authority when making decisions about the purchase of new computer technologies	No Answer	Not useful	Useful	Very useful	Do not use
Recommend only	0.00%	38.46%	46.15%	7.69%	7.69%
Need approval	9.09%	9.09%	27.27%	45.45%	9.09%
Have authority to buy	9.09%	18.18%	45.45%	18.18%	9.09%

Table 25.7.3 Usefulness of Print Handouts Describing Library Technology in educating patrons about computer technology in the library Broken out by Carnegie Class

Carnegie Class	No Answer	Not useful	Useful	Very useful	Do not use
Community College	0.00%	7.14%	42.86%	35.71%	14.29%
4-Year College	0.00%	50.00%	33.33%	0.00%	16.67%
MA/PHD Granting Institution	10.00%	30.00%	40.00%	20.00%	0.00%
Research University	20.00%	20.00%	40.00%	20.00%	0.00%

Table 25.7.4 Usefulness of Print Handouts Describing Library Technology in educating patrons about computer technology in the library Broken out by Public Versus Private

Public Versus Private	No Answer	Not useful	Useful	Very useful	Do not use
Public	4.17%	16.67%	45.83%	25.00%	8.33%
Private	9.09%	36.36%	27.27%	18.18%	9.09%

Table 25.7.5 Usefulness of Print Handouts Describing Library Technology in educating patrons about computer technology in the library Broken out by Total Annual Enrollment

Total Annual Enrollment	No Answer	Not useful	Useful	Very useful	Do not use
2,000 or less	0.00%	12.50%	37.50%	25.00%	25.00%
2,000 – 10,000	6.25%	31.25%	31.25%	25.00%	6.25%
More than 10,000	9.09%	18.18%	54.55%	18.18%	0.00%

Table 25.7.6 Usefulness of Print Handouts Describing Library Technology in educating patrons about computer technology in the library Broken out by Total Annual Tuition

Total Annual Tuition	No Answer	Not useful	Useful	Very useful	Do not use
Less than $5,000	0.00%	7.69%	30.77%	46.15%	15.38%
$5,000 - $20,000	10.00%	30.00%	50.00%	0.00%	10.00%
More than $20,000	8.33%	33.33%	41.67%	16.67%	0.00%

Table 25.8.1 Usefulness of Virtual Reference Systems or Instant Messaging in educating patrons about computer technology in the library

	No Answer	Not useful	Somewhat useful	Useful	Very useful	Do not use
Entire sample	5.71%	34.29%	5.71%	22.86%	14.29%	17.14%

Table 25.8.2 Usefulness of Virtual Reference Systems or Instant Messaging in educating patrons about computer technology in the library Broken out by Level of authority when making decisions about the purchase of new computer technologies

Level of authority when making decisions about the purchase of new computer technologies	No Answer	Not useful	Somewhat useful	Useful	Very useful	Do not use
Recommend only	0.00%	38.46%	7.69%	23.08%	23.08%	7.69%
Need approval	9.09%	27.27%	0.00%	18.18%	9.09%	36.36%
Have authority to buy	9.09%	36.36%	9.09%	27.27%	9.09%	9.09%

Table 25.8.3 Usefulness of Virtual Reference Systems or Instant Messaging in educating patrons about computer technology in the library Broken out by Carnegie Class

Carnegie Class	No Answer	Not useful	Somewhat useful	Useful	Very useful	Do not use
Community College	0.00%	50.00%	0.00%	28.57%	14.29%	7.14%
4-Year College	0.00%	33.33%	16.67%	33.33%	0.00%	16.67%
MA/PHD Granting Institution	10.00%	30.00%	10.00%	10.00%	20.00%	20.00%
Research University	20.00%	0.00%	0.00%	20.00%	20.00%	40.00%

Table 25.8.4 Usefulness of Virtual Reference Systems or Instant Messaging in educating patrons about computer technology in the library Broken out by Public Versus Private

Public Versus Private	No Answer	Not useful	Somewhat useful	Useful	Very useful	Do not use
Public	4.17%	41.67%	4.17%	25.00%	12.50%	12.50%
Private	9.09%	18.18%	9.09%	18.18%	18.18%	27.27%

Table 25.8.5 Usefulness of Virtual Reference Systems or Instant Messaging in educating patrons about computer technology in the library Broken out by Total Annual Enrollment

Total Annual Enrollment	No Answer	Not useful	Somewhat useful	Useful	Very useful	Do not use
2,000 or less	0.00%	50.00%	0.00%	25.00%	25.00%	0.00%
2,000 – 10,000	6.25%	31.25%	6.25%	18.75%	12.50%	25.00%
More than 10,000	9.09%	27.27%	9.09%	27.27%	9.09%	18.18%

Table 25.8.6 Usefulness of Virtual Reference Systems or Instant Messaging in educating patrons about computer technology in the library Broken out by Total Annual Tuition

Total Annual Tuition	No Answer	Not useful	Somewhat useful	Useful	Very useful	Do not use
Less than $5,000	0.00%	46.15%	0.00%	30.77%	7.69%	15.38%
$5,000 - $20,000	10.00%	40.00%	10.00%	20.00%	10.00%	10.00%
More than $20,000	8.33%	16.67%	8.33%	16.67%	25.00%	25.00%

Chapter 5. Outsourcing

Table 25.9 If your library outsources any computer or workstation information technology functions, such as maintenance or repairs, describe why you do this and what results that you have achieved. Point out savings in cost or increases in effectiveness. Do you use outside workstation maintenance services?

1. No, not outside the university. Campus IT maintains our computers.
2. Our ILS is serviced by the vendor while we host the servers in our racks.
3. We outsource about 95% of our public workstations to a central IT shop on campus. This provides a common environment for students across campus and at a lesser cost than when we handled the support ourselves. The students also have access to more applications/software in line with the courses they are enrolled in.
4. All maintenance provided by University IT Services, housed in the same building.
5. IT handles all this.
6. The Community college had an IT department with IT techs.
7. All is done in-house by college MIS department, which is not part of the library.
8. Apple support is outsourced.
9. Our IT department is entirely separate from the library. We have to formally request assistance, which is a drain of time, since they usually try to walk us through trouble-shooting the problem, if possible, even if we have already attempted to do so.
10. The university's Division of Technology Services deal with computers and workstation maintenance and repairs.
11. We purchase all machines with 3-year warrantees, which our campus computer store honors. It is more cost-effective for us to take machines in need of repair to them, so our staff can continue to do other work.
12. Do not use. Have looked into switching completely to a leasing setup but costs are much higher since we keep our hardware in service for much longer than the typical business life cycle (because of insufficient budget)
13. Our internal college IT department services our computers.
14. No - IT provides maintenance services.
15. IT dept. takes care of this function. Yes they buy the outside maintenance. The dept. will take care of it up to a point but as soon as it is a hardware issue, they will send it out to get if fixed. Most of the time. Network issues are different.
16. Our IT dept. handles maintenance.
17. Do not use outside workstation maintenance services.
18. We outsource our maintenance and repairs. This has saved us time and money as we are a small school with an IT department of one servicing all students, staff and faculty.
19. The college IT department does hardware related maintenance and repair, because they have an entire department of people and spare parts, etc. I'm not

sure if that would be considered outsourcing. The Systems Librarian does software-related maintenance and repairs. I am not sure how cost-saving these measures are, because we have no alternative to compare them to.

Chapter 6. Information Commons and Computer Centers

Table 26.1 Does your library have one or more computer centers or information technology centers in the library?

	No Answer	Yes	No
Entire sample	5.71%	65.71%	28.57%

Table 26.2 Does your library have one or more computer centers or information technology centers in the library? Broken out by Level of authority when making decisions about the purchase of new computer technologies

Level of authority when making decisions about the purchase of new computer technologies	No Answer	Yes	No
Recommend only	0.00%	61.54%	38.46%
Need approval	9.09%	63.64%	27.27%
Have authority to buy	9.09%	72.73%	18.18%

Table 26.3 Does your library have one or more computer centers or information technology centers in the library? Broken out by Carnegie Class

Carnegie Class	No Answer	Yes	No
Community College	0.00%	85.71%	14.29%
4-Year College	0.00%	16.67%	83.33%
MA/PHD Granting Institution	10.00%	60.00%	30.00%
Research University	20.00%	80.00%	0.00%

Table 26.4 Does your library have one or more computer centers or information technology centers in the library? Broken out by Public Versus Private

Public Versus Private	No Answer	Yes	No
Public	4.17%	79.17%	16.67%
Private	9.09%	36.36%	54.55%

Table 26.5 Does your library have one or more computer centers or information technology centers in the library? Broken out by Total Annual Enrollment

Total Annual Enrollment	No Answer	Yes	No
2,000 or less	0.00%	75.00%	25.00%
2,000 – 10,000	6.25%	56.25%	37.50%
More than 10,000	9.09%	72.73%	18.18%

Table 26.6 Does your library have one or more computer centers or information technology centers in the library? Broken out by Total Annual Tuition

Total Annual Tuition	No Answer	Yes	No
Less than $5,000	0.00%	84.62%	15.38%
$5,000 - $20,000	10.00%	70.00%	20.00%
More than $20,000	8.33%	41.67%	50.00%

Table 27.1 In your library or library system, how many complexes of computers or workstations would you say might be described as "information commons" or "computer centers" of some kind?

	Mean	Median	Minimum	Maximum
Entire sample	21.93	1.00	0.00	500.00

Table 27.2 In your library or library system, how many complexes of computers or workstations would you say might be described as "information commons" or "computer centers" of some kind? Broken out by Level of authority when making decisions about the purchase of new computer technologies

Level of authority when making decisions about the purchase of new computer technologies	Mean	Median	Minimum	Maximum
Recommend only	9.75	1.00	0.00	82.00
Need approval	2.13	2.00	0.00	6.00
Have authority to buy	52.40	1.50	0.00	500.00

Table 27.3 In your library or library system, how many complexes of computers or workstations would you say might be described as "information commons" or "computer centers" of some kind? Broken out by Carnegie Class

Carnegie Class	Mean	Median	Minimum	Maximum
Community College	8.67	1.00	0.00	82.00
4-Year College	4.40	1.00	0.00	20.00
MA/PHD Granting Institution	56.78	2.00	0.00	500.00
Research University	5.25	3.50	2.00	12.00

Table 27.4 In your library or library system, how many complexes of computers or workstations would you say might be described as "information commons" or "computer centers" of some kind? Broken out by Public Versus Private

Public Versus Private	Mean	Median	Minimum	Maximum
Public	29.90	1.00	0.00	500.00
Private	3.33	1.00	0.00	20.00

Table 27.5 In your library or library system, how many complexes of computers or workstations would you say might be described as "information commons" or "computer centers" of some kind? Broken out by Total Annual Enrollment

Total Annual Enrollment	Mean	Median	Minimum	Maximum
2,000 or less	1.71	1.00	0.00	6.00
2,000 – 10,000	8.21	1.00	0.00	82.00
More than 10,000	59.00	3.00	0.00	500.00

Table 27.6 In your library or library system, how many complexes of computers or workstations would you say might be described as "information commons" or "computer centers" of some kind? Broken out by Total Annual Tuition

Total Annual Tuition	Mean	Median	Minimum	Maximum
Less than $5,000	8.75	1.00	0.00	82.00
$5,000 - $20,000	2.89	2.00	0.00	12.00
More than $20,000	58.56	1.00	0.00	500.00

Table 27.7 Do you think that your library will be increasing or decreasing the number of these centers over the next few years? Increasing their resources or reducing them? What is your philosophy on their development? Will you stand pat? Make major change? How have tablets, netbooks and laptops affected your computer centers?

1. We'll be creating a research commons that includes a substantial number of computers in our new building--the library will have about 330 computers available for patrons, and about 120 will be grouped together in the research commons, the rest scattered around the building. Campus IT will have a help desk in the research commons.
2. Information commons is quite different from a computer center. Libraries will be shifting to the information commons in the next 10 years and away from computer centers.
3. We will increase resources in the near future to meet demand. I expect the use of small personal devices to increase, decreasing the need for campus computers labs.
4. No. Restricted by location.
5. I don't anticipate increasing the number of centers but we do plan on adding more machines to several of the centers. Portable devices don't appear to have lessened the demand for fixed workstations.
6. May be decreasing number of total desktop computers, but not number of centers. Tablets are not strong productivity tools. Increasing use of personal laptops will likely cause the decrease in desktops.
7. We are anticipating a remodel in the next few years that would enable us to have another computer lab area. Our desktop machines tend to be completely full in the mornings - checkout of laptops hasn't changed that.
8. We plan to maintain our labs and teaching spaces and possibly decrease amount of walk up computers in public areas
9. Budget limitations prohibit much expansion of technology in any form.
10. Same number of centers. Reducing resources. Development will be based upon student needs. We are making a major change now as we are moving by July to the Learning Commons model. Laptops are heavily used, tablets not so much as they require much more maintenance and training of students. Netbooks are a device whose time has come and gone.
11. We will increase the number of computers within the library. Computer labs outside the library proper are maintained by IT but no assistance is given to users.
12. Will likely stay the same due to budgetary constraints. Perhaps add a few more tablets, but otherwise no major renovations or additions.
13. We are a tiny school. We are still working in a 60 year old + building with major issues. We have much larger things to try to correct HVAC, electrical grid, asbestos. We will try to keep the terminals/laptops as up to date as we can, but much more than that is going to be a stretch.
14. Increasing. We want to have an information commons instead of just a grouping of computers; need buy in from Division of Technology Services

15. We will watch usage carefully. While most students have their own laptops, they still prefer to use our lab machines because of the wide variety of software packages on these machines (e.g. Photoshop, Sibelius, SPSS, etc.) that they could not afford to purchase themselves.
16. 2 centers are run by campus IT, the student body has not yet reached a tipping point on wireless/personal devices so labs may decrease slightly but probably not a lot in next couple of years. Library owned/maintained public computers are very likely to decrease down to only specialized workstations (Chinese/Japanese/Korean, ADA, etc.) because more users are virtual and more students bring their own laptops
17. Our students want both a lab and computers scattered through the building, so that's our goal.
18. We do not have a formal "computer center" in the library. There is one computer center on campus in a separate building. We have 50 public access workstations for students to use. We hope to add more workstations in the future but have maxed out our infrastructure (space, electrical, technology) capacity and have no budget for upgrades at this time.
19. We will keep our desktops and laptops, but add tablets and/or netbooks. May phase out desktop as other options become available, but it is an unknown at this point.
20. Increasing. Collaborative learning means more of these spaces. Renovated library space will have more group work rooms with smart boards, etc.
21. Maintain what we have, no increases.
22. Increasing and there will be no change in the computer centers as only PCs are planned for purchase.
23. Our computer labs are in the garden level of the library but they are not part of the library nor the academic-side of administration so that's a separate dept. that we have little to no knowledge of in terms of planning
24. Entire Library thought of as one large commons. New addition a BYOD commons, wireless, fully electrified.
25. No changes; no staff, no time, no funding.
26. Decreasing but will still maintain at least one.
27. I would like to offer more 'out of the room' accessibility for our resources, but I don't think that is a change that is in the works officially. I believe we will stay at our current level, perhaps grow by 10-15 workstations.
28. Decreasing in favor of mobile devices. We would not decrease resources available to patrons, but we would change the nature (e.g. replace desktops with laptops). My philosophy is to try to offer the most modern technology that we can within our budget. Laptops and tablets have already affected our computer centers -- we get a lot of patrons come in with their own devices. They are able to go anywhere in the library (some even sit on the floor). If these patrons did not come in with their own devices, then there would be lines of people waiting to use the desktops we provide.
29. We hope to increase one of the workstation areas, but building infrastructure limitations (electrical outlet and internet connection) limit the number of workstations we can have.

Table 27.8 How heavily are your computer centers used? What are the most popular types of hardware and software?

1. Internet, Word, Excel.
2. Usually 50-100% occupied.
3. Use depends on location. The library is the most heavily used for computing on campus.
4. Very heavily. Office, Photoshop (and other adobe products).
5. Compared to the other ~2,500-3,000 public computers on campus those in the library consistently rank as the most heavily used. Dell PC, MS Office suite and select software driven by course curriculum.
6. Occupancy rate in library during open hours is 87%. Most popular software: browser (IE, Safari, Firefox), MS Office (Word, PowerPoint, Excel--in that order).
7. Our computer labs are full Monday to Thursday mornings. MS Word and our online databases are the most popular software.
8. Again, all our students have laptops and iPads.
9. Computer centers are used heavily for Reference and Instruction sessions. Most popular is MS Office, Adobe, Firefox.
10. Heavy between classes.
11. Used pretty consistently - Word processing, printing.
12. Microsoft Office products are heavily used for writing papers. Excel is also used. Computer center is used by students doing research and by students and community patrons who do not have internet access at home, for work, school, and personal purposes.
13. Approximately 2,600 visitors a week. Most popular is based upon what the college standard computers are made available to students. The most popular are Apple products.
14. Very heavily-MS Word, Excel, and PowerPoint, AutoCAD.
15. Very heavily, Macs are most popular and Microsoft Office SPSS.
16. Moderately. Heaviest use is in Word processing, Microsoft Office products, and internet access.
17. We have heavy usage of our machines, especially during certain times of year. At some points it is mainly checking e-mail/Facebook. At other points we can fill up the building with people using the Microsoft suite products. Some usage of SPSS and other disciplinary programs too.
18. Our computer labs are used daily. Microsoft Office and Web browsers are our most popular software. We do have scanners that people use. Most people use our Dells; we only have 3 Macs.
19. Very heavily used - the library's computer labs get the heaviest use of any on campus. 50/50 split of Dell and Apple machines. Office suite is still the favored software, along with SPSS and Photoshop.
20. Very heavily used most of the semester. Dell hardware for same reason - statewide contract.
21. Fairly heavily. All hardware is the same. They use word and the internet.
22. Our 50 public workstations are used heavily throughout the day. Students most

commonly use MS Office software and printing (via GoPrint).

23. Completely full at certain times during the semester. Microsoft suite, but also Canvas, our learning management system.
24. Busy all year long. Microsoft Word and PowerPoint are the most heavily used software.
25. Right before classes start and MS software and psych test scoring software.
26. Very heavily. PCs.
27. The computer labs are not used much at all except for by faculty teaching larger classes.
28. Very - Microsoft & Adobe products most popular.
29. Heavily. Dell PCs standard Microsoft package.
30. Very heavily used. Microsoft office and some specialized programs for specific classes.
31. They are used heavily all day long. The popular hardware are scanners and printers; popular software are MS Office; Photoshop, illustrator, Adobe professional.
32. Very heavily - from the moment we open to the moment we close we always have students using them. Our scanners are in constant demand. Photoshop, Illustrator and 3DS Max are often used programs. Microsoft Office is also very popular. And of course - general internet browsing.
33. Fairly heavily. We only offer PCs with either Windows XP or Windows 7, depending on the location.
34. Very heavily during mid-day when most classes are beginning and ending.

Table 28.1 Which phrase best describes the library's efforts to make library resources available through tablets, smartphones and other hand held technologies:

	No Answer	We have not done much in this area	We have not done much but are studying it and plan to do more soon	We have already made some provisions for access to some library resources through tablets and smartphones	We have numerous applications in place to allow for library resource access through many different types of tablets and smartphones
Entire sample	5.71%	28.57%	11.43%	48.57%	5.71%

Table 28.2 Which phrase best describes the library's efforts to make library resources available through tablets, smartphones and other hand held technologies: Broken out by Level of authority when making decisions about the purchase of new computer technologies

Level of authority when making decisions about the purchase of new computer technologies	No Answer	We have not done much in this area	We have not done much but are studying it and plan to do more soon	We have already made some provisions for access to some library resources through tablets and smartphones	We have numerous applications in place to allow for library resource access through many different types of tablets and smartphones
Recommend only	0.00%	15.38%	15.38%	61.54%	7.69%
Need approval	9.09%	36.36%	9.09%	45.45%	0.00%
Have authority to buy	9.09%	36.36%	9.09%	36.36%	9.09%

Table 28.3 Which phrase best describes the library's efforts to make library resources available through tablets, smartphones and other hand held technologies: Broken out by Carnegie Class

Carnegie Class	No Answer	We have not done much in this area	We have not done much but are studying it and plan to do more soon	We have already made some provisions for access to some library resources through tablets and smartphones	We have numerous applications in place to allow for library resource access through many different types of tablets and smartphones
Community College	0.00%	35.71%	14.29%	42.86%	7.14%
4-Year College	0.00%	50.00%	16.67%	33.33%	0.00%
MA/PHD Granting Institution	10.00%	10.00%	10.00%	60.00%	10.00%
Research University	20.00%	20.00%	0.00%	60.00%	0.00%

Table 28.4 Which phrase best describes the library's efforts to make library resources available through tablets, smartphones and other hand held technologies: Broken out by Public Versus Private

Public Versus Private	No Answer	We have not done much in this area	We have not done much but are studying it and plan to do more soon	We have already made some provisions for access to some library resources through tablets and smartphones	We have numerous applications in place to allow for library resource access through many different types of tablets and smartphones
Public	4.17%	33.33%	8.33%	45.83%	8.33%
Private	9.09%	18.18%	18.18%	54.55%	0.00%

Table 28.5 Which phrase best describes the library's efforts to make library resources available through tablets, smartphones and other hand held technologies: Broken out by Total Annual Enrollment

Total Annual Enrollment	No Answer	We have not done much in this area	We have not done much but are studying it and plan to do more soon	We have already made some provisions for access to some library resources through tablets and smartphones	We have numerous applications in place to allow for library resource access through many different types of tablets and smartphones
2,000 or less	0.00%	50.00%	25.00%	25.00%	0.00%
2,000 – 10,000	6.25%	18.75%	12.50%	56.25%	6.25%
More than 10,000	9.09%	27.27%	0.00%	54.55%	9.09%

Table 28.6 Which phrase best describes the library's efforts to make library resources available through tablets, smartphones and other hand held technologies: Broken out by Total Annual Tuition

Total Annual Tuition	No Answer	We have not done much in this area	We have not done much but are studying it and plan to do more soon	We have already made some provisions for access to some library resources through tablets and smartphones	We have numerous applications in place to allow for library resource access through many different types of tablets and smartphones
Less than $5,000	0.00%	30.77%	15.38%	46.15%	7.69%
$5,000 - $20,000	10.00%	20.00%	10.00%	50.00%	10.00%
More than $20,000	8.33%	33.33%	8.33%	50.00%	0.00%

Table 29 How much has the library spent on smartphone technology in the past two years? How much do you think you will spend cumulatively over the next two years?

Table 29.1.1 Amount spent on smartphone technology in the Past Two Years

	Mean	Median	Minimum	Maximum
Entire sample	$578.67	$0.00	$0.00	$15,000.00

Table 29.1.2 Amount spent on smartphone technology in the Past Two Years Broken out by Level of authority when making decisions about the purchase of new computer technologies

Level of authority when making decisions about the purchase of new computer technologies	Mean	Median	Minimum	Maximum
Recommend only	$27.69	$0.00	$0.00	$350.00
Need approval	$0.00	$0.00	$0.00	$0.00
Have authority to buy	$2,125.00	$0.00	$0.00	$15,000.00

Table 29.1.3 Amount spent on smartphone technology in the Past Two Years Broken out by Carnegie Class

Carnegie Class	Mean	Median	Minimum	Maximum
Community College	$26.92	$0.00	$0.00	$350.00
4-Year College	$0.00	$0.00	$0.00	$0.00
MA/PHD Granting Institution	$251.25	$0.00	$0.00	$2,000.00
Research University	$3,750.00	$0.00	$0.00	$15,000.00

Table 29.1.4 Amount spent on smartphone technology in the Past Two Years Broken out by Public Versus Private

Public Versus Private	Mean	Median	Minimum	Maximum
Public	$826.67	$0.00	$0.00	$15,000.00
Private	$0.00	$0.00	$0.00	$0.00

Table 29.1.5 Amount spent on smartphone technology in the Past Two Years Broken out by Total Annual Enrollment

Total Annual Enrollment	Mean	Median	Minimum	Maximum
2,000 or less	$43.75	$0.00	$0.00	$350.00
2,000 – 10,000	$153.85	$0.00	$0.00	$2,000.00
More than 10,000	$1,667.78	$0.00	$0.00	$15,000.00

Table 29.1.6 Amount spent on smartphone technology in the Past Two Years Broken out by Total Annual Tuition

Total Annual Tuition	Mean	Median	Minimum	Maximum
Less than $5,000	$29.17	$0.00	$0.00	$350.00
$5,000 - $20,000	$1,888.89	$0.00	$0.00	$15,000.00
More than $20,000	$1.11	$0.00	$0.00	$10.00

Table 29.2.1 Anticipated cumulative spending on smartphone technology over the Next Two Years

	Mean	Median	Minimum	Maximum
Entire sample	$943.08	$0.00	$0.00	$20,000.00

Table 29.2.2 Anticipated cumulative spending on smartphone technology over the Next Two Years Broken out by Level of authority when making decisions about the purchase of new computer technologies

Level of authority when making decisions about the purchase of new computer technologies	Mean	Median	Minimum	Maximum
Recommend only	$47.27	$0.00	$0.00	$500.00
Need approval	$0.00	$0.00	$0.00	$0.00
Have authority to buy	$3,000.00	$0.00	$0.00	$20,000.00

Table 29.2.3 Anticipated cumulative spending on smartphone technology over the Next Two Years Broken out by Carnegie Class

Carnegie Class	Mean	Median	Minimum	Maximum
Community College	$41.67	$0.00	$0.00	$500.00
4-Year College	$0.00	$0.00	$0.00	$0.00
MA/PHD Granting Institution	$670.00	$0.00	$0.00	$4,000.00
Research University	$5,000.00	$0.00	$0.00	$20,000.00

Table 29.2.4 Anticipated cumulative spending on smartphone technology over the Next Two Years Broken out by Public Versus Private

Public Versus Private	Mean	Median	Minimum	Maximum
Public	$1,226.00	$0.00	$0.00	$20,000.00
Private	$0.00	$0.00	$0.00	$0.00

Table 29.2.5 Anticipated cumulative spending on smartphone technology over the Next Two Years Broken out by Total Annual Enrollment

Total Annual Enrollment	Mean	Median	Minimum	Maximum
2,000 or less	$62.50	$0.00	$0.00	$500.00
2,000 – 10,000	$444.44	$0.00	$0.00	$4,000.00
More than 10,000	$2,224.44	$0.00	$0.00	$20,000.00

Table 29.2.6 Anticipated cumulative spending on smartphone technology over the Next Two Years Broken out by Total Annual Tuition

Total Annual Tuition	Mean	Median	Minimum	Maximum
Less than $5,000	$41.67	$0.00	$0.00	$500.00
$5,000 - $20,000	$3,000.00	$0.00	$0.00	$20,000.00
More than $20,000	$3.33	$0.00	$0.00	$20.00

Chapter 8. Patron Policies

Table 29.3 What is your library's peak use period for computer workstations and what do you do during these times, if anything, to serve patrons as best you can?

1. Sunday through Thursday evenings from about 6 pm to midnight. We don't do anything extra.
2. 11 am to 2 pm and 8 pm to midnight.
3. Mid-morning to 10:00 pm, Sunday through Thursdays. We reserve computers for student use only.
4. Beginning of semester and finals weeks. Mornings, noon, and late afternoon.
5. Peak times are early mornings and early afternoons on class days. We simply try to direct patrons to more of the out of the way computer locations.
6. Peak times: Monday –Thursday, 11:00 a.m.-3:00 p.m. Sunday to Wednesday, 7:00 p.m.-11:p.m. Sunday, 1:00 p.m.-5:00 p.m. No special additional services, other than staffing patterns at help desks.
7. Monday to Thursday, 8 a.m. to 12:30 pm. If there are people waiting to use a computer, we ask everyone who is not doing schoolwork to leave and come back later. This works pretty well. We also do not allow guests to use the computers until after 2 p.m.
8. Peak use is any day between 4 pm and 11 pm. Peak times during the year are study periods before exams (November and April).
9. When the library opens before class, between classes, especially around noon, and just before 6 p.m. classes. We look for students who look like they need help.
10. Finals week.
11. Mondays, Wednesdays, and Fridays, 9.a.m. to 1 p.m., following the flow of class times. We try to keep two staffers at the desk to answer questions at peak use times.
12. 9am - 3pm and 6pm - 8pm, Monday to Thursday.
13. 4 pm to 8 pm. We direct students to other computer labs when we are full and tell students to move from specialized engineering computers when they are needed by the engineering students.
14. Finals, lots of printers.
15. Varies based on the point in the semester, but generally the 1 - 4pm time is a heavy period.
16. We are on semesters. September and early October we are packed. We have a robust first-year student orientation program. Paper times: early-mid November and early-mid April. Finals time: mid-December and late April.
17. 11 am to 2 pm.

18. Monday to Wednesday, 10am – 8pm.
19. 10am to 2pm -- we have made more tables with electrical outlets available for students who bring their own devices.
20. Our peak computer usage time is from 9 am until 5 pm Monday - Thursday. Our computers are on a first-come-first-serve basis. We do not monitor how much time someone has been using a computer nor what they are accessing on the computers. If not computers available in the library, we suggest students check out one of the library's nine laptops or go to the computer lab on campus.
21. Mornings, Monday - Thursday. Make sure we have coverage at both the Circulation and Reference Desk. Work Study students help with technology problems. They are terrific!
22. 10 am to 6 pm -- we try and ensure that machines are working and everyone at a PC is actually using it and just not sitting at it
23. 4 -7pm and place paper in the copy machine and fix copy machine problems!
24. 10 am -2 pm. We bought more desktops to accommodate the students.
25. Fluctuates throughout the day, depending on the break between classes. Afternoon tends to see more consistently heavy use.
26. Probably evenings/nights. Most students bring their own laptops. I haven't heard of many complaints that students couldn't get to a computer if they needed one.
27. 100% peak.
28. 10 am-2 pm. Run around a lot.
29. March and October are the peak use periods. We have a classroom with computers and we open that for use too when the library is very busy.
30. Middle of the day is the peak time: 11 am -2 pm.
31. 10am - 6pm; we are usually full with a waiting list. We try to limit computer use to academic uses only. We have a number of computer labs on campus we can direct them to if they want to mess about.
32. Probably between 3:00 to 6:00 PM. We don't do anything special, but we are heavily staffed during that time.
33. Our peak times are in the afternoon. We have no process related to them and provide little management of them.

Table 30 In the following years, approximately what percentage of library patrons predominantly use their own computers while at the library rather than those supplied by the library itself?

Table 30.1.1 Percentage of library patrons who use their own computers in 2011

	Mean	Median	Minimum	Maximum
Entire sample	25.72%	20.00%	1.50%	95.00%

Table 30.1.2 Percentage of library patrons who use their own computers in 2011 Broken out by Level of authority when making decisions about the purchase of new computer technologies

Level of authority when making decisions about the purchase of new computer technologies	Mean	Median	Minimum	Maximum
Recommend only	25.38%	20.00%	5.00%	95.00%
Need approval	38.13%	30.00%	5.00%	95.00%
Have authority to buy	15.17%	10.00%	1.50%	50.00%

Table 30.1.3 Percentage of library patrons who use their own computers in 2011 Broken out by Carnegie Class

Carnegie Class	Mean	Median	Minimum	Maximum
Community College	21.38%	15.00%	3.00%	95.00%
4-Year College	18.00%	7.50%	2.00%	55.00%
MA/PHD Granting Institution	33.33%	25.00%	5.00%	95.00%
Research University	30.38%	35.00%	1.50%	50.00%

Table 30.1.4 Percentage of library patrons who use their own computers in 2011 Broken out by Public Versus Private

Public Versus Private	Mean	Median	Minimum	Maximum
Public	21.89%	20.00%	1.50%	95.00%
Private	36.25%	20.00%	5.00%	95.00%

Table 30.1.5 Percentage of library patrons who use their own computers in 2011 Broken out by Total Annual Enrollment

Total Annual Enrollment	Mean	Median	Minimum	Maximum
2,000 or less	25.38%	12.50%	3.00%	95.00%
2,000 – 10,000	30.58%	20.00%	2.00%	95.00%
More than 10,000	20.15%	15.00%	1.50%	50.00%

Table 30.1.6 Percentage of library patrons who use their own computers in 2011 Broken out by Total Annual Tuition

Total Annual Tuition	Mean	Median	Minimum	Maximum
Less than $5,000	24.83%	17.50%	3.00%	95.00%
$5,000 - $20,000	19.83%	20.00%	1.50%	50.00%
More than $20,000	32.78%	15.00%	5.00%	95.00%

Table 30.2.1 Percentage of library patrons who use their own computers in 2012-13

	Mean	Median	Minimum	Maximum
Entire sample	34.10%	30.00%	2.00%	95.00%

Table 30.2.2 Percentage of library patrons who use their own computers in 2012-13 Broken out by Level of authority when making decisions about the purchase of new computer technologies

Level of authority when making decisions about the purchase of new computer technologies	Mean	Median	Minimum	Maximum
Recommend only	35.25%	32.50%	8.00%	95.00%
Need approval	41.67%	30.00%	10.00%	90.00%
Have authority to buy	25.00%	25.00%	2.00%	50.00%

Table 30.2.3 Percentage of library patrons who use their own computers in 2012-13 Broken out by Carnegie Class

Carnegie Class	Mean	Median	Minimum	Maximum
Community College	29.83%	30.00%	8.00%	90.00%
4-Year College	30.40%	25.00%	2.00%	65.00%
MA/PHD Granting Institution	40.56%	25.00%	15.00%	95.00%
Research University	37.00%	40.00%	3.00%	65.00%

Table 30.2.4 Percentage of library patrons who use their own computers in 2012-13 Broken out by Public Versus Private

Public Versus Private	Mean	Median	Minimum	Maximum
Public	30.38%	30.00%	2.00%	90.00%
Private	42.78%	25.00%	10.00%	95.00%

Table 30.2.5 Percentage of library patrons who use their own computers in 2012-13 Broken out by Total Annual Enrollment

Total Annual Enrollment	Mean	Median	Minimum	Maximum
2,000 or less	35.63%	30.00%	10.00%	90.00%
2,000 – 10,000	35.92%	30.00%	2.00%	95.00%
More than 10,000	30.11%	30.00%	3.00%	65.00%

Table 30.2.6 Percentage of library patrons who use their own computers in 2012-13 Broken out by Total Annual Tuition

Total Annual Tuition	Mean	Median	Minimum	Maximum
Less than $5,000	33.91%	30.00%	8.00%	90.00%
$5,000 - $20,000	28.89%	30.00%	2.00%	50.00%
More than $20,000	39.00%	22.50%	10.00%	95.00%

Table 31.1 For how many mobile devices is the library capable of providing both electricity and internet access?

	Mean	Median	Minimum	Maximum
Entire sample	2,142.47	50.00	0.00	15,000.00

Table 31.2 For how many mobile devices is the library capable of providing both electricity and internet access? Broken out by Level of authority when making decisions about the purchase of new computer technologies

Level of authority when making decisions about the purchase of new computer technologies	Mean	Median	Minimum	Maximum
Recommend only	151.89	25.00	0.00	1,000.00
Need approval	51.67	50.00	0.00	150.00
Have authority to buy	9,757.50	12,000.00	30.00	15,000.00

Table 31.3 For how many mobile devices is the library capable of providing both electricity and internet access? Broken out by Carnegie Class

Carnegie Class	Mean	Median	Minimum	Maximum
Community College	46.88	27.50	0.00	150.00
4-Year College	26.00	26.00	2.00	50.00

MA/PHD Granting Institution	4,018.57	60.00	0.00	1,5000.00
Research University	6,075.00	6,075.00	150.00	12,000.00

Table 31.4 For how many mobile devices is the library capable of providing both electricity and internet access? Broken out by Public Versus Private

Public Versus Private	Mean	Median	Minimum	Maximum
Public	3,117.31	100.00	0.00	15,000.00
Private	30.33	35.00	0.00	60.00

Table 31.5 For how many mobile devices is the library capable of providing both electricity and internet access? Broken out by Total Annual Enrollment

Total Annual Enrollment	Mean	Median	Minimum	Maximum
2,000 or less	21.25	22.50	10.00	30.00
2,000 – 10,000	57.75	50.00	0.00	150.00
More than 10,000	5,737.14	1,000.00	0.00	15,000.00

Table 31.6 For how many mobile devices is the library capable of providing both electricity and internet access? Broken out by Total Annual Tuition

Total Annual	Mean	Median	Minimum	Maximum

Tuition				
Less than $5,000	59.29	30.00	0.00	150.00
$5,000 - $20,000	6,030.00	6,050.00	20.00	12,000.00
More than $20,000	2,021.50	50.00	0.00	15,000.00

Table 31.7 Going forward how do you anticipate that use of patron's own mobile devices in the library will impact your library's computer purchasing plans?

1. We will be buying large monitors that students can use with their own devices, particularly for group work. I suppose demand will go down for circulating mobile devices, unless we put specialized software on them. And even then, I expect we'll be going to web-based access for software eventually.
2. Purchasing additional computers will lessen.
3. Yes, we will likely switch to lower cost terminals that access a virtual desktop infrastructure.
4. Unknown at this point; it will be interesting to see. We anticipate increased mobile use, but it has not affected desktop use at this point. It is common to see a mobile in use by a desktop user at the same time.
5. We may be able to reduce our purchase of both laptop and desktop machines.
6. The amount of public walk up computers may decrease.
7. We will not replace all the PCs.
8. Still trying to figure this one out.
9. We will most likely replace existing computer workstations, but add more seating and electrical service for mobile devices, all of which seem to need to be charged at the same time.
10. Possibly. We are an urban community college where many students do not have technology readily available to them or they cannot afford such technology.
11. We have little power in purchasing. The administration seems to believe that students will increasingly supply their own devices, but our non-traditional student are often very low income and cannot afford to do this.
12. More electricity and workstations.
13. We would like to provide better charging areas and more comfortable spaces for those with their own devices.

14. Again, we have a lot of issues here. Looking at a 10 year major renovation plan. At that point, we'll have to make some big changes.
15. Not much since our users surprisingly are still gravitating towards our computer labs, even when they bring or own their own laptops. A number of our students who check out laptops mention they actually own their own laptop but they still use our service.
16. Yes, but it is difficult to predict at this point in time.
17. We have not budget to purchase technology at this time.
18. At this time, no impact.
19. Library manager does not anticipate/plan for these issues.
20. I think we will purchase more kinds of computers but fewer in number total.
21. It will decrease our computer purchasing plans.
22. Minimally - again the programs we provide are cost prohibitive for personal purchase and require powerful machines to run.
23. If we see that the majority of patrons have their own devices, then this will greatly impact purchasing plans. Currently that is not the case, but we expect this might change in the next few years.
24. We may finally get Wi-Fi in the next year, so that will likely change this paradigm significantly.
25. We haven't considered this yet.

www.ingramcontent.com/pod-product-compliance
Lightning Source LLC
LaVergne TN
LVHW061246100826
845148LV00008B/1042

* 9 7 8 1 5 7 4 4 0 2 4 9 0 *